Beginner's
Dari

(Persian)

Hippocrene Beginner's Series

Arabic
Armenian
Assyrian
Basque
Bulgarian
Chinese
Czech
Dari (Persian)
Dutch
French
Greek
Hungarian
Irish
Italian
Japanese
Lithuanian
Maori
Persian
Polish
Romanian
Russian
Scottish Gaelic
Serbo-Croatian
Shona (ChiShona)
Sicilian
Slovak
Spanish
Turkish
Vietnamese
Welsh

Beginner's Dari

(Persian)

Shaista Wahab

Hippocrene Books, Inc.
New York

I wish to thank Spozhmai Maiwandi for her insightful suggestions on improving the manuscript.

ISBN 0-7818-1012-4

For information, address:
Hippocrene Books, Inc.
171 Madison Avenue
New York, NY 10016

Cataloging-in-Publication data available from the Library of Congress.

Printed in the United States of America.

Contents

Part IV: Vocabulary

Part V: Greetings, Common Phrases, and Expressions

Introduction

The Constitution of 1964 established Dari and Pashto as the two official languages in Afghanistan. Most Afghans are bilingual and know both Dari and Pashto. Dari is an Indo-European language and uses the same alphabet as Arabic.

The Afghan government used Dari and Pashto for official transactions and business. Dari lost its importance after the Taliban took over Kabul in 1996, as the Taliban were mostly Pashto speakers. The interim government of Hamid Karzai that replaced the Taliban in December 2001 promotes both languages as the official languages of Afghanistan.

Dari is spoken by more than 50 percent of the total 22 million Afghans, and it is understood by over 90 percent of the population. In addition to Afghanistan, Dari or Persian is also used in Iran and Tajikistan. Afghanistan is a landlocked country in Central Asia. Bounded on the north by Tajikistan, Uzbekistan, and Turkmanistan, to the west by Iran, to the northeast by China, and to the east and southeast by Pakistan. Kabul is the capital of Afghanistan and is populated by more than 3 million. Other major cities in Afghanistan are Herat, Kandahar, Ghazni, Mazar-i Sharif, and Faiz Abad. A person from Afghanistan is called an Afghani or an Afghan. Afghani is also the name of the currency used in Afghanistan. One U.S. dollar is equal to approximately 50 Afghani.

The Dari language has several dialects in Afghanistan, and they are called Hazaragi, Tajiki, Heratis, Panjshiri, and Aimaqi. The various dialects of Dari language are similar enough for Dari speakers to understand each other. In this book, I have used the dialect used in Kabul called Kabuli Dari or Kabuli Farsi.

Dari, Farsi, Persian, and Tajiki are names referring to the same language. It is called Dari or Farsi in Afghanistan, Farsi or Persian in Iran, and Tajiki in Tajikistan. Different alphabets are used: in Tajikistan, the Cyrillic alphabet is used for Tajiki, while speakers in Afghanistan and Iran use the Arabic script. A slight variation of dialect and pronunciation of some words exists in these countries. Some Arabic words were introduced in Dari due to the influence of Islam.

Once you become familiar with the Dari alphabet, reading and writing will become easy. The Dari alphabet contains 32 letters; 28 of the 32 are used in Arabic. The four Dari letters not in Arabic are: پ *pe*, چ *che*, گ *g*, and ژ *zhe*.

Throughout the book, I have transliterated Dari words with the Roman alphabet to provide a pronunciation guide. Transliterating a language into the Roman alphabet is not an easy task because a few Dari letters do not have equivalent sounds in English, and no Roman letter is a good representation of those sounds.

How to Use This Book

Set a goal for yourself and decide how much time you want to devote to the study of the Dari language. The best way to learn is to study daily. You may not be able to finish one lesson every day; spend as much time as you need. Do not go to the next lesson until you have learned all the words and have understood the material from your current one. It is very important that you learn a lesson thoroughly before starting the next one.

The first part of the book teaches you the Dari alphabet. As you learn the alphabet, you also learn new Dari words in each lesson. Follow the instructions and complete the exercises in each lesson. Pronounce letters and words to familiarize yourself with the sound of Dari. After you have learned the alphabet, try to read the Dari writings without looking at the transliterations. Each lesson has a vocabulary list that includes new words; study these to build your vocabulary.

The book is divided into five parts, each part designed to help you learn the Dari language systematically. Part one consists of seven lessons that teach reading, writing, and pronunciation of the Dari alphabet. You should be able to read and write the Dari alphabet without difficulty by the end of this section. Part two consists of ten lessons that teach you the basic rules of Dari. In this section, you learn the essential Dari rules, about things like gender and articles one needs to know when acquiring the language. Part three is designed to familiarize you with basic grammar and sentence construction. Minimum grammar instructions about elements like verbs and prepositions are given to introduce you to basic Dari rules. Part four teaches numbers, colors, months, and other basic vocabulary. Follow the instructions and learn new words and their pronunciation.

Parts one through four are designed to teach reading, writing, and speaking of the Dari language. Part five can be used independently from the rest of the book. This section is designed to help you while you are in Afghanistan by teaching you common questions and expressions, allowing you to converse with the locals. The pronunciation of Dari words and letters are in *italic* script throughout the book.

Part I

Writing

Dari Alphabet (الفبای دری)

ا ب پ ت ث ج چ ح خ د ذ ر ز ژ س ش ص ض
ط ظ ع غ ف ق ک گ ل م ن و ه ی

The Dari alphabet has thirty-two letters. These letters can occur at the beginning, at the middle or at the end of a word. The initial short form of a letter is used when it occurs at the beginning of a word and it is joined with the letter that follows it. The letters ا *alef,* د *d`al,* ذ *z`al,* ر *re,* ز *ze,* ژ *zhe,* and و *vav* are always written in their full or long forms. When these letters appear in the middle of a word, they will not connect to the letters that follow them. However, they may join with their preceding letters. The remaining Dari letters are written in their short forms when they occur in the middle of a word and are joined by their preceding and following letters.

Dari has three letters for the sound of *s,* two letters for the sound of *t,* three letters for *h,* and four letters for *z.* I did not distinguish between the various forms of letters s, t, h, and z in transliterating the Dari words into English; however, all Dari words are written with their proper Dari spellings.

Alphabet		Initial (short form)	Medial (short form)	Terminal (long form)	Transcription
ا	alef	ا		ا	a, `a, e, i, o, u
ب	be	ب	ب	ب	b
پ	pe	پ	پ	پ	p
ت	te	ت	ت	ت	t
ث	se	ث	ث	ث	s
ج	jeem	ج	ج	ج	j
چ	che	چ	چ	چ	ch
ح	he	ح	ح	ح	h
خ	khe	خ	خ	خ	kh
د	d`al	د		د	d
ذ	z`al	ذ		ذ	z
ر	re	ر		ر	r
ز	ze	ز		ز	z
ژ	zhe	ژ		ژ	zh
س	seen	س	س	س	s
ش	sheen	ش	ش	ش	sh
ص	s`ad	ص	ص	ص	s
ض	z`ad	ض	ض	ض	z
ط	toy	ط	ط	ط	t
ظ	zoy	ظ	ظ	ظ	z
ع	ayn	ع	ع	ع	`
غ	ghayn	غ	غ	غ	gh
ف	fe	ف	ف	ف	f
ق	qaf	ق	ق	ق	q
ک	kaf	ک	ک	ک	k
گ	gaf	گ	گ	گ	g
ل	l`am	ل	ل	ل	l
م	meem	م	م	م	m
ن	nun	ن	ن	ن	n
و	vav	و		و	v, ow, w, u
ه	he	ه	ه	ه	h
ی	ya	ی	ی	ی	y, i, ei

Vowels

`a`	as in walk	*n`an*	نا ن	bread
a	as in march	*mard*	مر د	man
e	as in earth	*esm*	اسم	name
i	as in sit	*ins`an*	انسا ن	human
o	as in do	*dony`a*	دنیا	world
`u`	as in sue	*t`ut*	توت	mulberry

Consonants

These letters are pronounced the same as in English:

b d f g h j k l m n p q r s t v y z

The combination of two English letters makes the sound of the following Dari letters:

kh	خ	as in German Bach
sh	ش	as in shoe
ch	چ	as in chair
zh	ژ	as in measure
gh	غ	No similar sound found in English. It sounds like a thick *r* in French. The sound comes from the back of the throat while the tongue touches the front of the roof of the mouth behind the upper teeth.

Lesson One اول درس

The Letter ا *alef*

An initial *alef* always stands alone. ا *alef* attaches to connecting letters that precede it. Short forms of *alef* are transcribed as a, e, i, o, u and the long form of *alef* as `a.

| اسپ | (short form) | *asp* | (as in fast) | horse |
| بار | (long form) | *b`ar* | (as in far) | load |

In بار *b`ar* the letter *alef* is connected to the preceding letter ب *be*. When *alef* appears in the middle of a word, it does not connect to the following letter.

The initial long *alef* آ (`a) signifies a long `a. It is called آ *alef mad*. The mark above the *alef* is called *mad*. When long ا *alef* comes in the middle of a word it will not require the *mad* above it. For example the ا *alef* in بار *b`ar* is a long ا *alef* without a *mad* above it.

آب	`ab	water
آسان	`as`an	easy
آینده	`ayenda	future

When ل *l`am* is followed by ا *alef*, the combination of both letters is called *l`am alef l`a*. It is written as لا. It is pronounced *l`a*.

لاله	l`alah	tulip
سلام	sal`am	hello
پلان	pl`an	plan

alef is written as a straight line. To write *alef* start from the top and move down.

Exercise تمرین

Write the ا *alef* several times. Pronounce as you write. Start from the right side of the page and move to the left as you write. Dari is written from right to the left.

ا *alef* ا ا ا ا ا ا ا ا ا ا ا

Write the following words. Pronounce as you write. Find their meanings in the list at the end of the chapter.

`ab آب آب آب آب آب

`as`an آسان آسان آسان آسان آسان

`ayenda آینده آینده آینده آینده آینده

asp اسپ اسپ اسپ اسپ اسپ

b`ar بار بار بار بار بار

l`alah لاله لاله لاله لاله لاله

sal`am سلام سلام سلام سلام سلام

pl`an پلان پلان پلان پلان پلان

Vocabulary

آسان	`as`an	easy
آینده	`ayenda	future
سلام	sal`am	hello
اسپ	asp	horse
بار	b`ar	load
پلان	pl`an	plan
لاله	l`alah	tulip
آب	`ab	water

Lesson Two   درس دوم

Letters ب *be* through خ *khe*

These letters may connect to the letters before or after them: ب *be*, پ *pe*, ت *te*, ث *se*, ج *jeem*, چ *che*, ح *he*, and خ *khe*. Other letters that act similarly are: س *seen*, ش *sheen*, ص *s`ad*, ض *z`ad*, ط *toy*, ظ *zoy*, ع *ayn*, غ *ghayn*, ف *fe*, ق *qaf*, ک *kaf*, گ *gaf*, ل *l`am*, م *meem*, ن *nun, and* ی *ya*. You will learn these in future lessons.

The letters ب *be*, پ *pe*, ت *te*, and ث *se* are all written alike. The differences between them are the number of dots that are placed above or below these letters. ب *be* has one dot below it, پ *pe* has three dots below it, ت *te* has two dots above it, and ث *se* has three dots above it.

When these letters are terminal letters in a word, they are written in their long forms. When they join with following or preceding letters, they are written in their short forms. To write these letters start from the right corner and make the downward curve. Move your pen to the left and then up to complete your writing.

تمرین Exercise

Write the following letters. Pronounce as you write.

ب	ب	ب	ب	ب	ب	ب	ب	ب	ب	*be*
پ	پ	پ	پ	پ	پ	پ	پ	پ	پ	*pe*
ت	ت	ت	ت	ت	ت	ت	ت	ت	ت	*te*
ث	ث	ث	ث	ث	ث	ث	ث	ث	ث	*se*

Write the following words. Pronounce as you write. Find their meanings in the list at the end of the chapter.

بابا بابا بابا بابا بابا بابا بابا بابا بابا *b`ab`a*

باغ باغ باغ باغ باغ باغ باغ باغ *b`agh*

بام بام بام بام بام بام بام بام *b`am*

پنیر پنیر پنیر پنیر پنیر پنیر پنیر پنیر *panir*

پیر پیر پیر پیر پیر پیر پیر پیر *pir*

تربوز تربوز تربوز تربوز تربوز تربوز تربوز تربوز *tarb`uz*

توت توت توت توت توت توت توت توت *t`ut*

Letters ج *jeem,* ج *che,* ح *he,* and خ *khe* are all written alike. The distinctions between them are the number of dots and their placement in these letters. ج *jeem* has one dot in the middle, ج *che* has three dots in the middle, ح *he* has no dot, and خ *khe* has one dot above it. When these letters are terminal letters in a word, they are written in their long forms. When they precede or are followed by connecting letters they are written in their short forms. To write these letters start from the top left corner of these letters, move to right and then down from left to right, a counterclockwise move.

Exercise تمرین

Write the following letters. Pronounce as you write.

ج	ج	ج	ج	ج	ج	ج	ج	ج	ج	*jeem*
چ	چ	چ	چ	چ	چ	چ	چ	چ	چ	*che*
ح	ح	ح	ح	ح	ح	ح	ح	ح	ح	*he*
خ	خ	خ	خ	خ	خ	خ	خ	خ	خ	*khe*

Write the following words. Pronounce as you write. Find their meanings in the list at the end of the chapter.

جگ جگ جگ جگ جگ جگ جگ جگ						*jag*
چای چای چای چای چای چای چای						*ch`ai*
حویلی حویلی حویلی حویلی حویلی حویلی						*hawaili*
خانه خانه خانه خانه خانه خانه خانه						*kh`ana*

Vocabulary

باغ	*b`agh*	garden
بابا	*b`ab`a*	father
بام	*b`am*	roof
پنیر	*panir*	cheese
پیر	*pir*	old
تربوز	*tarb`uz*	watermelon
توت	*t`ut*	mulberry
جگ	*jag*	pitcher
خانه	*kh`ana*	home
چای	*ch`ai*	tea
حویلی	*hawaili*	yard

Lesson Three   درس سوم

Letters د *d`al* through ش *sheen*

Letters د *d`al,* ذ *z`al,* ر *re,* ز *ze,* and ژ *zhe* are non-medial connecting letters. When these letters appear in the middle of a word, they will not connect to letters that follow them. However, they may connect to preceding letters.

The letters د *d`al* and ذ *z`al* are written alike. To write these letters start from the top, move your pen down and make the curve. Add the dot above ذ *z`al* last. The distinction between them is that د *d`al* has no dot and ذ *z`al* has one dot above it.

Exercise   تمرین

Write the letters د *d`al* and ذ *z`al* several times. Read aloud as you write.

d`al   د   د   د   د   د   د   د   د   د   د   د   د   د
z`al   ذ   ذ   ذ   ذ   ذ   ذ   ذ   ذ   ذ   ذ   ذ   ذ   ذ

Write the following words. As always pronounce as you write, and find their meanings in the list at the end of this chapter.

diw`ar   دیوار دیوار دیوار دیوار دیوار دیوار دیوا دیوار
zarah   ذره   ذره   ذره   ذره   ذره   ذره   ذره   ذره

The letters ر *re,* ز *ze,* and ژ *zhe* are written alike. The distinctions between them are the number of dots used in these letters. ر *re* has no dot, ز *ze* has one dot above it, and ژ *zhe* has three dots above it. To write these letters start from the top and move down to make the curve. The curve is not as deep as in the letter د *d`al* and the letter ذ *z`al.*

Exercise تمرین

Write these letters.

ر	ر	ر	ر	ر	ر	ر	ر	ر	*re*
ز	ز	ز	ز	ز	ز	ز	ز		*ze*
ژ	ژ	ژ	ژ	ژ	ژ	ژ	ژ		*zhe*

Write the following words. (Are you pronouncing them as you write?)

رابر رابر رابر رابر رابر رابر رابر رابر *r`abar*
زرد زرد زرد زرد زرد زرد زرد *zard*
ژاله ژاله ژاله ژاله ژاله ژاله ژاله *zh`alah*

The letters س *seen* and ش *sheen* can be written with three teeth or with a long line. When س *seen* and ش *sheen* are initial or medial letters, they are written in their short forms. All three teeth would be of equal size, like ـسـ and ـشـ. If they are the terminal letters in a word, they will keep their long or full forms, even when they are connected to preceding letters. The distinction between س *seen* and ش *sheen* is that س *seen* has no dot and ش *sheen* has three dots above it.

تمرین Exercise

Write the following letters.

seen	س س س س س س س س س س
sheen	ش ش ش ش ش ش ش ش ش ش

Write the following words. (Have you found their meanings in the list at the end of the chapter?)

sirka	سرکه سرکه سرکه سرکه سرکه سرکه سرکه
shutur	شتر شتر شتر شتر شتر شتر شتر

Vocabulary

سرکه	*sirka*	vinegar
ژاله	*zh`alah*	hail
زرد	*zard*	yellow
رابر	*r`abar*	rubber
ذره	*zarah*	particle, an atom
دیوار	*diw`ar*	wall
شتر	*shutur*	camel

Lesson Four درس چهارم

Letters ص s`ad through ظ zoy

The letters ص s`ad and ض z`ad are written alike. The difference between them is that ص has no dot and ض has one dot above it. To write ص s`ad and ض z`ad, start with ض or ص and then move down clockwise. When ص s`ad and ض z`ad are initial or medial letters they are written in their short forms. When they are terminal letters, they keep their long forms.

Exercise تمرین

Write the following letters.

s`ad   ص ص ص ص ص ص ص ص ص ص
z`ad   ض ض ض ض ض ض ض ض ض ض

Write the following words.

s`aboon   صابون صابون صابون صابون صابون صابون صابون
zarar   ضرر ضرر ضرر ضرر ضرر ضرر ضرر

The letters ط *toy* and ظ *zoy* may connect to their preceding or following connecting letters. The letters ط and ظ are always written in their full forms, regardless of their position in the word. To write these letters start with the bottom part of the letters and move clockwise. Then add the straight line. To add the straight line, start from top and move down.

تمرين Exercise

Write the following letters.

ط ط ط ط ط ط ط ط ط ط ط *toy*

ظ ظ ظ ظ ظ ظ ظ ظ ظ ظ ظ *zoy*

Write the following words.

طرف طرف طرف طرف طرف طرف طرف طرف *taraf*

خط خط خط خط خط خط خط *khat*

ظهر ظهر ظهر ظهر ظهر ظهر ظهر ظهر *zuhr*

Vocabulary

صابون	*s`aboon*	soap
ظهر	*zuhr*	afternoon
طرف	*taraf*	toward, side, in direction of
خط	*khat*	letter, writing, line
ضرر	*zarar*	damage

Lesson Five   درس پنجم

Letters ع *ayn* through ق *qaf*

The letters ع *ayn* and غ *ghayn* may connect to connecting letters that proceed them or letters that follow them. To write ع or غ start from the top and move counter clockwise. When these letters are initial or medial letters in a word, they are written in their short forms. When they are terminal letters, they are written in their long forms.

تمرین Exercise

Write the following letters.

ع	ع	ع	ع	ع	ع	ع	ع	ع	ع	*ayn*
غ	غ	غ	غ	غ	غ	غ	غ	غ	غ	*ghayn*

Write the following words.

علم	علم	علم	علم	علم	علم	علم	*'ilm*
معلم	معلم	معلم	معلم	معلم	معلم	معلم	*mu`alim*
غم	غم	غم	غم	غم	غم	غم	*gham*
باغ	باغ	باغ	باغ	باغ	باغ	باغ	*b`agh*

The letter ف *fe* can be connected to a preceding or a following letter. When ف *fe* is the initial or medial letter in a word, it is written in its short form. When it appears as a terminal letter, it is written in its long form.

To write the letter ف *fe* start from right and move to the left. Add the dot last.

تمرین Exercise

Write the letter ف *fe*

fe ف ف ف ف ف ف ف ف

Write the following words.

farm`an فرمان فرمان فرمان فرمان فرمان فرمان فرمان

faq`ir فقیر فقیر فقیر فقیر فقیر فقیر فقیر

`aft`ab آفتاب آفتاب آفتاب آفتاب آفتاب آفتاب آفتاب آفتاب

barf برف برف برف برف برف برف برف برف

The letter ق *qaf* can connect to the preceding or following connecting letter in a word. When ق *qaf* is the initial or medial letter in a word, it is written in its short form. When it appears as a terminal letter in a word, it is written in its long form. Write the letter ق *qaf* from right to the left.

Exercise تمرین

Write the letter ق *qaf*.

qaf   ق   ق   ق   ق   ق   ق   ق

Write the following words.

qalam   قلم   قلم   قلم   قلم   قلم   قلم

qasr   قصر   قصر   قصر   قصر   قصر   قصر

bairaq   بیرق   بیرق   بیرق   بیرق   بیرق   بیرق

barq   برق   برق   برق   برق   برق   برق

Vocabulary

علم	`ilm	knowledge
معلم	mu`alim	teacher
غم	gham	sadness
باغ	b`agh	garden
فرمان	farm`an	decree
فقیر	faq`ir	beggar
آفتاب	`aft`ab	sun
برف	barf	snow
قلم	qalam	pen
قصر	qasr	palace
بیرق	bairaq	flag
برق	barq	electricity

Lesson Six   درس ششم

Letters ک *kaf* through ن *n`un*

The letters ک *kaf* and گ *gaf* are written alike. The difference between them is that گ *gaf* has an extra slash above it. When these letters appear as initial or medial letters, they are written in their short forms. When they are terminal letters, they are written in their long forms. Write ک *kaf* and گ *gaf* from right to the left.

تمرین Exercise

Write the following letters.

ک	ک	ک	ک	ک	ک	ک	ک	ک	ک	ک	*kaf*
گ	گ	گ	گ	گ	گ	گ	گ	گ	گ	گ	*gaf*

Write the following words.

کتاب کتاب کتاب کتاب کتاب کتاب کتاب کتاب *kit`ab*
کار کار کار کار کار کار کار *k`ar*
مکتب مکتب مکتب مکتب مکتب مکتب مکتب *maktab*
سرک سرک سرک سرک سرک سرک سرک *sarak*
برگ برگ برگ برگ برگ برگ برگ *barg*
سگ سگ سگ سگ سگ سگ سگ *sag*

The letter ل *lam* may connect to its preceding letter or to connecting letters that follow it. When ل is the initial or medial letter in a word, it is written in its short form. When ل is the terminal letter in a word it will keep its long form. To write the letter ل you start from the upper right end of the letter ل and move your pen clockwise to complete the half circle.

تمرین Exercise

Write the following letter.

lam ل   ل   ل   ل   ل   ل   ل   ل   ل   ل

Write the following words.

l`alah لاله لاله لاله لاله لاله لاله لاله لاله

lashkar لشکر لشکر لشکر لشکر لشکر لشکر لشکر

bale بلی بلی بلی بلی بلی بلی بلی بلی

feel فیل فیل فیل فیل فیل فیل فیل فیل

gul گل گل گل گل گل گل گل گل

The letter م *meem* may connect to its preceding or following letter. When م appears as the initial or medial letter, it is written in its short form. When م appears as the terminal letter it will keep its long form. To write م *meem*, start at the top and move down.

تمرین Exercise

Write the letter م *meem* several times.

م م م م م م م م م م *meem*

Write the following Dari words.

magas مگس مگس مگس مگس مگس مگس مگس
morcha مورچه مورچه مورچه مورچه مورچه مورچه مورچه
man من من من من من من من
namak نمک نمک نمک نمک نمک نمک نمک
komak کمک کمک کمک کمک کمک کمک کمک
garm گرم گرم گرم گرم گرم گرم گرم
gom گم گم گم گم گم گم گم

The letter ن n'un may connect to a preceding or following letter. When ن is the initial or medial letter in a word, it will be written in its short form. When it is the final letter in a word it will be written in its long form. To write ن n'un start at the right end of ن and move clockwise. Add the dot last.

تمرین Exercise

Write the letter ن n'un as below.

ن ن ن ن ن ن ن ن ن ن ن *n'un*

Write the following Dari words.

نمک نمک نمک نمک نمک نمک نمک *namak*

نان نان نان نان نان نان نان نان *n'an*

نام نام نام نام نام نام نام *n'am*

انسان انسان انسان انسان انسان انسان انسان انسان *ins'an*

زن زن زن زن زن زن زن زن *zan*

Vocabulary

مورچه	*morcha*	ant
مگس	*magas*	fly
گل	*gul*	flower
فیل	*feel*	elephant
بلی	*bale*	yes
لشکر	*lashkar*	army
لاله	*l`alah*	tulip
سگ	*sag*	dog
برگ	*barg*	leaf
سرک	*sarak*	street
مکتب	*maktab*	school
کار	*k`ar*	work
کتاب	*kit`ab*	book
گم	*gom*	lost
گرم	*garm*	warm
کمک	*komak*	help
نمک	*namak*	salt
من	*man*	I
زن	*zan*	women
نام	*n`am*	name
انسان	*ins`an*	human
نان	*n`an*	bread

Lesson Seven   درس هفتم

Letters و vav through ی ya

The letter و vav can connect with a preceding letter but not to a following letter. vav is always written in its full form. To write و vav, start from top, make the small head, and move down to complete the curve.

تمرین Exercise

Write the letter و vav several times. (Have you been pronouncing as you write?)

vav و   و   و   و   و   و   و

Write the following words.

vaqt وقت   وقت   وقت   وقت   وقت   وقت

toshak توشک   توشک   توشک   توشک   توشک   توشک

gosht گوشت   گوشت   گوشت   گوشت   گوشت   گوشت

tu تو   تو   تو   تو   تو   تو

du دو   دو   دو   دو   دو   دو

The letter ه *he* attaches to preceding and following letters in a word. It changes its written form depending on the location of the letter, whether at the beginning, the ending or in the middle.

Initial:	هوا	*hav`a*	weather	
Medial:	آنها	*`anh`a*	they	
Terminal:	نقشه	*naqshah*	map	(Terminal *he* preceded by a connecting letter)
Terminal:	بوره	*b`urah*	sugar	(Terminal *he* preceded by a non-connecting letter)

تمرین Exercise

Write the following words. (Have you been finding their meanings in the list at the end of the chapter?)

hav`a   هوا هوا هوا هوا هوا هوا هوا هوا

`anh`a   آنها آنها آنها آنها آنها آنها آنها آنها

naqshah   نقشه نقشه نقشه نقشه   نقشه نقشه نقشه

b`urah   بوره بوره بوره بوره بوره بوره بوره

The letter ی *ya* changes its written form depending on the location of the letter as it appears in a word. It is written in short form when it is an initial letter and is followed by a connecting letter, or when it is a medial letter preceded and followed by connecting letters. The short ـیـ *ya* is written as a short ـبـ *be*, with two dots below it instead of the one dot as in ـبـ *be*. ی *ya* usually keeps its long form when it connects to a preceding letter and also when it is the terminal letter in a word, or when it is the terminal letter in a word and is preceded by a non-connecting letter.

یک	*yak*	initial letter ی followed by connecting letter ک.
بینی	*b'ini*	medial letter ی preceded by letter ب and followed by letter ن.
آبی	*'abi*	terminal letter ی preceded by connecting letter ب.
بوی	*boe*	terminal letter ی preceded by non-connecting letter و.

Exercise تمرین

Write the following words.

yak   یک یک یک یک یک یک یک یک

b'ini   بینی بینی بینی بینی بینی بینی، بینی

'abi   آبی آبی آبی آبی آبی آبی آبی آبی

boe   بوی بوی بوی بوی بوی بوی بوی

Vocabulary

بینی	*b`ini*	nose
دو	*du*	two
تو	*tu*	you
گوشت	*gosht*	meat
توشک	*toshak*	mattress
وقت	*vaqt*	time
بوره	*b`urah*	sugar
نقشه	*naqshah*	map
هوا	*hav`a*	weather
آنها	*`anh`a*	they
یک	*yak*	one
آبی	*`abi*	blue
بوی	*boe*	smell

Part II

Rules

Lesson Eight   درس هشتم

Writing Dari

Dari is written from right to left. The Dari language does not use capitalization; proper names and the first letters of sentences are not capitalized as in English.

In writing Dari, pen strokes are usually from top to bottom. For example if you write the word اسم *esm*, you begin with the letter ا *alef*. Start from the top of the letter ا *alef* and pull down a straight line to write the letter ا *alef*. Then write the letter س *seen* starting from the right end of the letter س *seen* and add the letter م *meem* to it. The tail end of م *meem* is where you complete writing this word. It takes two pen strokes to write the word اسم. One stroke is for ا and the second stroke is for سم.

When ا *alef* is connected to a preceding letter, the pen stroke for ا *alef* starts at the base of the letter to which *alef* ا connects and moves straight upward. For example if you write the word بار *b`ar*, you start with the short form of the letter ب *be*, then attach the letter ا *alef* to it at the left end of the letter ب *be* with a straight upward move to write the letter ا *alef*. The letter ر *re* is added last. Add the dot below the ب *be* last. When writing Dari add the dots after you complete writing a word.

When ا *alef* is written separately, the pen stroke is from top to bottom. When ا *alef* joins a preceding letter, the pen stroke starts from the base of the letter to which it connects and moves upward.

تمرین Exercise

Write the following words to practice your Dari.

esm اسم اسم اسم اسم اسم اسم اسم اسم اسم

'in این این این این این این این این این

'an آن آن آن آن آن آن آن آن آن

k`ak`a کاکا کاکا کاکا کاکا کاکا کاکا کاکا کاکا کاکا

m`am`a ماما ماما ماما ماما ماما ماما ماما ماما ماما

n`am نام نام نام نام نام نام نام نام نام

Write the following in Dari. Pronounce as you write. Remember their English meanings.

این مرد	*'in mard*	this man
آن مرد	*'an mard*	that man
نقشه آبی	*naqshah-e[1] 'abi*	blue map
یک نقشه	*yak naqshah*	one map
یک مرد	*yak mard*	one man
آن نقشه	*'an naqshah*	that map
اسم من	*esm-e man*	my name
نام من	*n`am-e man*	my name
نام او or اسم او[2]	*n`am-e o* or *esm-e o*	his name

Write the following sentences in Dari. Pronounce as you write.

نام من شیلا است.	*n`am-e man Sheila ast.*	My name is Sheila.
نام او حسن است.	*n`am-e o Hasan ast.*	His name is Hasan.
آن مرد کاکا من است.	*'an mard k`ak`a-e man ast.*	
		That man is my uncle.
این نقشه آبی است.	*'in naqshah 'abi ast.*	This map is blue.
نام او مریم است.	*n`am-e o Mariyam ast.*	Her name is Mariyam.

---

[1] See Lesson Twelve: "*Ez`afa* or the addition '-e'"

[2] There is no difference in the usage of اسم esm or نام n`am, they are completely interchangeable.

Vocabulary

مرد	*mard*	man
نام	*n`am*	name
ماما	*m`am`a*	uncle (mother's brother)
کاکا	*k`ak`a*	uncle (father's brother)
آن	*`an*	that
این	*`in*	this
اسم	*esm*	name
است	*ast*	is

Lesson Nine درس نهم

و *vav* "and"

The letter و *vav* is pronounced *va* when it is used in a sentence and when it means "and" as in English. و *va* is written separately and will not join with following and preceding words when it is used to denote the word "and." و *vav* is added before the last noun even when a sentence has more than two nouns.

کتاب و قلم	*kit`ab va qalam*	book **and** pen
دختر و بچه	*dokhtar va bacha*	girl **and** boy
سیاه و سفید	*sey`a va safed*	black **and** white

من کتاب، قلم و کتابچه خریدم.
man kit`ab, qalam va kit`abcha khar`idam.
I bought book, pen, and notebook.

شیلا، حسن و صوفی به مکتب رفتند.
Sheil`a, Hassan, va, Sophi beh maktab raftand.
Sheila, Hassan, and Sophi went to school.

Exercise تمرین

Write the following Dari phrases. As always pronounce as you write, and find their English meanings.

نقشه و کتاب
سیاه و سفید
دختر و بچه
قلم و کتاب

Write the following sentences in Dari.

شیلا یک قلم آبی و یک کتابچه خرید.
Sheil`a yak qalam-e `abi va yak kit`abcha khar`id.
Sheila bought a blue pen and a notebook.

او به دکان به همرای مادر، خواهر و برادر خود رفت.
o beh dok`an beh hamr`aey m`adar, khw`ahar va ber`ader-e khud raft.
He went to the store with his mother, sister and brother.

این کتاب سفید من و آن قلم آبی من است.
`in kit`ab-e safed-e man va `an qalam-e `abi-e man ast.
This is my white book and that is my blue pen.

او یک برادر و یک خواهر دارد.
o yak ber`ader va yakkhw`ahar d`arad.
He has a brother and a sister.

Vocabulary

کتاب	*kit`ab*	book
قلم	*qalam*	pen
دختر	*dokhtar*	girl
بچه	*bacha*	boy
و	*va*	and
سیاه	*sey`ah*	black
سفید	*safed*	white
نقشه	*naqshah*	map
مکتب	*maktab*	school
کتابچه	*kit`abcha*	notebook
دکان	*dok`an*	store
همرای	*hamr`ay*	with
خرید	*khar`id*	bought
برادر	*ber`ader*	brother
خواهر	*khw`ahar*	sister
مادر	*m`ader*	mother

درس دهم Lesson Ten

را r`a to Denote a Definite Direct Object

را r`a is a particle added to Dari nouns and comes after the noun to denote that it is the definite direct object. را  r`a is usually added as a suffix to the definite object by context or by the presence of a pronoun or name. را r`a can be used after personal pronouns: من را دید  *man r`a d`id* (saw me) or تو را دید  *t`u r`a d`id* (saw you).

You can write من and تو and را separate or together as one word.

Both forms of writing are acceptable in Dari. Omit the ن from من and attach the ر to م in order to write مرا *man r`a* as one word. Omit the و from تو and add the ر to ت in order to write ترا  *tu r`a* as one word.

من را *man r`a* or  مرا  *mar`a*
تو را *t`u r`a* or ترا *tur`a*

او مرا دعوت کرد.	*o mar`a da`wat kard.*	He invited me.
من ترا دیدم.	*man t`ur`a d`idam.*	I saw you.
حسن معلم را دید.	*Hasan mu`alim r`a d`id.*	Hasan saw the teacher.
حسن کتاب را خرید.	*Hasan kit`ab r`a khar`id.*	Hasan bought the book.
حسن مکتوب را خواند.	*Hasan makt`ub r`a khw`and.*	Hasan read the letter.
حسن او را دید.	*Hasan o r`a d`id.*	Hasan saw him/her.

When a sentence has more than one definite noun that relates to a direct object, a را *r`a* is added after the final noun. را *r`a* is used only once, even if the sentence has more than one noun.

حسن کتاب و قلم را خرید
Hasan kit`ab va qalam r`a khar`id.
Hasan bought the book and the pen.

حسن معلم و شاگرد را در مکتب دید.
Hasan mu`alim va sh`agird r`a dar maktab d`id.
Hasan saw the teacher and the student at school.

من یک قلم و یک کتابچه را برای مکتب خریدم.
man yak qalam va yak kit`abcha r`a bar`ay maktab kharidam.
I bought a pen and a notebook for school.

In the above sentences, references are made to specific nouns. The speaker and the listener both know which teacher, which student, which book, which letter and which person that they are talking about. When the noun is not clear the speaker may add additional information to clarify it for the listener. Like:

من معلم دری را دیدم.
man mu`alim Dari r`a d`idam.
I saw the Dari teacher.

حسن کتاب دری را خرید.
Hasan kit`ab-e Dari r`a kharid.
Hasan bought the Dari book.

تمرین Exercise

Read and write the following Dari sentences.

من معلم را دیدم.
man mu`alim r`a d`idam.
I saw the teacher.

معلم قلم آبی را خرید.
mu`alim qalam-e `abi r`a kharid.
The teacher bought the blue pen.

حسن نقشه را خرید.
Hasan naqsha r`a kharid.
Hasan bought the map.

او قلم و کتابچه را خرید.
o qalam va kit`abcha r`a kharid.
He bought the pen and the notebook.

او شاگرد را دید.
o sh`agird r`a d`id.
He saw the student.

Write the following Dari paragraph. Read as you write.

شیلا و حسن به دکان رفتند. شیلا یک قلم آبی را خرید. حسن یک قلم،
یک کتابچه و یک نقشه را خرید. حسن کاکا خود را در دکان دید.
شیلا و حسن در صنف دوم هستند.

Translation:
Sheila and Hasan went to the store. Sheila bought a blue pen. Hasan bought a pen, a notebook, and a map. Hasan saw his uncle in the store. Sheila and Hasan are in second grade.

Vocabulary

دری	*Dari*	Dar`i[3]
مکتوب	*makt`ub*	letter
خواند	*khw`and*	read
دید	*d`id*	saw
معلم	*mu`alim*	teacher
شاگرد	*sh`agird*	student
صنف دوم	*sinf-e duvum*	second grade
دعوت	*da`wat*	invite

---

[3] Dari is also known as Persian or Farsi.

Lesson Eleven درس یازدهم

Gender

Dari nouns have no gender distinction between masculine and feminine.
The gender becomes clear in the context of a statement or a sentence.

او پدر من است.
*o **pedar-e** man ast.*
He is my **father.**

او مادر من است.
o m`ader-e man ast.
She is my **mother.**

او مکتب را خوش دارد.
o maktab r`a khosh d`arad.
She likes school.

او مکتب را خوش دارد.
o maktab r`a khosh d`arad.
He likes school.

او معلم فزیک من است.
o mu'alim-e fiz`ik-e man ast.
He is my physics teacher.

تمرین Exercise

Write the following Dari paragraph, pronounce as you write.

مادر و پدر من هر دو معلم هستند. مادر من معلم دری است. او هر
روز به مکتب میرود.   مادر من بیست شاگرد در صنف خود دارد.
پدر من معلم انگلیسی است. پدر من معلم شیلا است. او در پوهنتون درس میدهد.

Translation:

My mother and my father, both are teachers. My mother is a Dari
teacher. She goes to school every day. My mother has twenty
students in her class. My father is an English teacher. My father is
Sheila's teacher. He teaches at the University.

Write the following Dari sentences.

نام معلم من حسن است.
n`am-e ma'alim-e man Hasan ast.
My teacher's name is Hasan.

من یک قلم خریدم.
man yak qalam kharidam.
I bought a pen.

صنف من چهار کلکین دارد.
sinf-e man chah`ar kilkeen d`arad.
My classroom has four windows.

مادر احمد معلم است.
m`ader-e Ahmad mu`alim ast.
Ahmad's mother is a teacher.

من بیست افغانی دارم.
man b`ist Afgh`ani d`aram.
I have twenty Afghanis.

او معلم من است.

o mu`alim-e man ast.

She is my teacher.

من فزیک را خوش دارم.

man fiz`ik r`a khosh d`aram.

I like physics.

شیلا مکتب رفت.

Sheila maktab raft.

Sheila went to school.

افغانستان میوه خشک زیاد دارد.

Afghanistan maywa-e khushk ziy`ad d`arad.

Afghanistan has a lot of dried fruits.

Vocabulary

بیست	*b`ist*	twenty
انگلیسی	*inglisi*	English
درس	*dars*	lesson
درس دادن	*dars d`adan*	to teach
پوهنتون	*pohant`un*	university
خوش	*khosh*	like
شاگرد	*sh`agird*	student
خواهر	*khw`ahar*	sister
مادر	*m`ader*	mother
پدر	*pedar*	father
فزیک	*fiz`ik*	physics
صنف	*sinf*	classroom
کلکین	*kilkeen*	window
چهار	*chah`ar*	four
میوه	*maywa*	fruit
خشک	*khushk*	dry
زیاد	*ziy`ad*	a lot, too much

Lesson Twelve درس دوازدهم

Ez`afa or the addition "-e", and Articles

In spoken Dari a non-stressed colloquial "-e" is an added sound at the end of all nouns that denotes a relationship between nouns and adjectives. This "-e" is called *ez`afa*, which means addition. In the context of a sentence, the "-e" sound is added to show one of the three relationships between the noun and the adjective.

i.   It indicates possession or belonging to:

برادر من	*ber`adar-e man*	My brother
خانه احمد	*khana-e Ahmad*	Ahmad's house

ii.   It joins a noun to an adjective that qualifies that noun:

قالین سرخ	*q`al`in-e surkh*	Red carpet
قلم سبز	*qalam-e sabz*	Green pen
سال نو	*s`al-e naw*	New Year

iii.   It indicates an apposition:

معلم، دوست او	*mu`alim, dost-e o*	The teacher, his friend
زن، همسایه من	*zan, hams`aya-e man*	The woman, my neighbor

The sound *ez`afa* "-e" is an added sound, but is not written in Dari.

Articles

The Dari language does not use the definite article "the" as in English.

دختر معلم به مکتب آمد.
dokhtar-e mu`alim beh maktab `amad.
The teacher's daughter came to school.

کتاب آبی اینجا است.
kit`ab-e `abi `inj`a ast.
The blue book is here.

قلم معلم بالا چوکی است.
qalam-e mu`alim b`al`a-e chawki ast.
The teacher's pen is on the chair.

شاگردان در صنف هستند.
sh`agird`an dar sinf hastand.
The students are in class.

تمرین Exercise

Write the following Dari sentences. Read as you write.

معلم حسن اینجا است.
mu`alim-e Hasan `inj`a ast.
Hasan's teacher is here.

او یک قالین سرخ خرید.
o yak q`al`in-e surkh kharid.
He bought a red carpet.

معلم در صنف است.
mu`alim dar sinf ast.
The teacher is in class.

نقشه بالا چوکی است.
naqshah b`al`a-e chawki ast.
The map is on the chair.

شاگرد کتاب را می خواند.
sh`agird kit`ab r`a may khw`anad.
The student is reading a book.

قالین سرخ است.
q`al`in surkh ast.
The carpet is red.

کاکا او به مکتب آمد.
k`k`a-e o beh maktab `amad.
His uncle came to school.

Vocabulary

همسایه	*hams`aya*	neighbor
زن	*zan*	woman
دوست	*dost*	friend
سال نو	*s`al-e naw*	new year
نو	*naw*	new
سال	*s`al*	year
سبز	*sabz*	green
قالین	*q`al`in*	carpet
خانه	*kh`ana*	house, home
برادر	*ber`adar*	brother
مگس	*magas*	fly
کتابخانه	*kit`abkh`ana*	library
هستند	*hastand*	are
صنف	*sinf*	classroom
شاگردان	*sh`agird`an*	students
شاگرد	*sh`agird*	student
چوکی	*chawk`i*	chair
بالا	*b`al`a*	over, above
آمد	*`amad*	came
اینجا	*`inj`a*	here
فزیک	*fiz`ik*	physics
به	*beh*	to
آفتاب	*`aft`ab*	sun
برف	*barf*	snow
مقبول	*maqbool*	pretty

Lesson Thirteen   درس سیزدهم

Statements, Questions, Commands, & Interrogative Sentences

A sentence consists of a number of words put together in an organized manner to convey a message. Also a sentence can be a command, an interrogative, a question, or a statement, and it could be negative or affirmative.

As a rule, subjects and objects come before the verbs in Dari sentences. Verbs usually appear last:

این کتاب من است
*'in kit`ab-e man **ast**.*
This **is** my book.

[The verb in the above sentence is *ast* است (**is**)]

پسر من مکتب رفت.
*pesar-e man maktab **raft**.*
My son **went** to school.

[In the above sentence *raft* رفت (**went**) is the verb.]

Statements

حسن خانه میآید.
Hasan kh`ana me`ayad.
Hasan comes home.

کتاب بالا میز است.
kit`ab b`al`a-e maiz ast.
The book is on the table.

حسن مکتب رفت.
Hasan maktab raft
Hasan went to school.

Questions

⁴ آیا حسن خانه آمد؟
`ay`a Hasan kh`ana `amad?
Did Hasan come home?

آیا کتاب بالا میز است؟
ay`a kit`ab b`al`a-e maiz ast?
Is the book on the table?

آیا حسن مکتب رفت؟
`ay`a Hasan matkab raft?
Did Hasan go to school?

In colloquial Dari, instead of using the word آیا *`ay`a*, a vocal stress is put at the end of the sentence to indicate a question. For example, removing the word آیا *`ay`a* and putting a vocal stress at the end of each sentence would not change their meaning.

حسن خانه میآید؟
Hasan kh`ana may`amad?
Did Hasan come home?

کتاب بالا میز است؟
kit`ab b`al`a-e maiz ast?
Is the book on the table?

حسن مکتب رفت؟
Hasan matkab raft?
Did Hasan go to school?

---

⁴   See Lesson Fourteen for using آیا *`ay`a*.

Commands

حسن ، خانه بیا.
Hasan, kh`ana bey`a.
Hasan, come home

حسن ، مکتب برو.
Hasan, maktab bero.
Hasan, go to school.

حسن، کتاب را بخوان.
Hasan, kit`ab r`a bekhw`an.
Hasan, read the book.

حسن، سیب را بخور.
Hasan, seb r`a bekhor.
Hasan, eat the apple.

شیلا، این کتاب را بخوان.
Sheila, `in kit`ab r`a behkhw`an.
Sheila, read this book.

شیلا، این فصل را بخوان.
Sheila, `in fasl r`a behkhw`an.
Sheila, read this chapter.

شیلا، این سیب را بخور.
Sheila, `in seb r`a behkhor.
Sheila, eat this apple.

شیلا، این صفحه رانوشته کن.
Sheila, `in safha r`a navishta kun.
Sheila, write this page.

شیلا، کتاب سرخ را بخر.
Sheila, kit`ab-e surkh r`a behkhar.
Sheila, buy the red book.

شیلا، به کتابخانه برو.
Sheila, beh kit`abkh`ana birau.
Sheila, go to the library.

Interrogatives

Interrogative questions are usually tonal, where a stress is placed on the last syllable. Interrogative questions normally begin with کجا *koj`a* (where), کی *k`i* (who or whom), چه *che* (what), کدام *kod`am* (which), and کی *kai* (when).[5]

کجا رفتی؟	*koj`a rafti?*	Where did you go?
کدام کتاب را خواندی.	*kod`am kit`ab r`a khw`andi?*	
		Which book did you read?
کی آمد؟	*k`i `amad?*	Who came?
چه خوردی؟	*che khord`i*	What did you eat?
کی آمدی؟	*kai `amadi?*	When did you come?

English sentences first translated to Dari, then changed to questions:

Sheila came home.
شیلا خانه آمد.
Sheila kh`ana `amad.

Did Sheila come home?
آیا شیلا خانه آمد؟
`ay`a Sheila kh`ana `amad?

Sheila went home.
شیلا خانه رفت
Sheila kh`ana raft.

Did Sheila go home?
آیا شیلا خانه رفت؟
`ay`a Sheila kh`ana raft?

Sheila saw the teacher.
شیلا معلم را دید·
Sheila mu'alim r`a d`id.

Did Sheila see the teacher?
آیا شیلا معلم را دید؟
`ay`a Sheila mu'alim r`a d`id?

Sheila bought a red pen.
شیلا یک قلم سرخ خرید·
Sheila yak qalam kharid.

Did Sheila buy a red pen?
آیا شیلا یک قلم سرخ خرید؟
`ay`a Sheila yak qalam surkh kharid?

Interrogative sentences:

چه خریدی؟	*che kharidi?*	What did you buy?
چه خواندی؟	*che khwandi?*	What did you read?
کجا رفتی؟	*koj`a rafti?*	Where did you go?
چه وقت آمدی؟	*che vaqt `amadi?*	When did you come?
کی بهمراه تو رفت؟	*k`i beh hamr`ah-e tu raft?*	Who went with you?
چه کردی؟	*che kardi?*	What did you do?

---

[5] کی *kai* and کی *k`i* are written alike. The difference between them is in their pronunciations and in their meanings.

Vocabulary

رفتن	*raftan*	to go
رفت	*raft*	went
برو	*birau*	go
سرخ	*surkh*	red
است	*ast*	is
من	*man*	I, my
دید	*d`id*	saw
در	*dar*	in
سر[6] or بالا	*sar* or *b`al`a*	on, above, over
کتابخانه	*kit`abkh`ana*	library
صفحه	*safha*	page
برادر	*ber`adar*	brother
آمدن	*`amadan*	to come
گپ زدن	*gapzadan*	to talk
گپ زد	*gapzad*	talked
با	*b`a*	with
بخوان	*bekhw`an*	read
کدام	*kod`am*	which
کی	*k`i*	who
چه	*che*	what
همراه	*hamr`ah*	with
کجا	*koj`a*	where
کردن	*kardan*	to do
فصل	*fasl*	chapter, season
کی	*kai*	when

---

[6] سر *sar* also means head.

Lesson Fourteen درس چهاردهم

Questions That Start With آیا `ay`a

آیا `ay`a is a particle used at the beginning of a non-interrogative sentence to introduce a question. It does not have any specific meaning. In conversational Dari, if a question is not interrogative in nature instead of using آیا `ay`a at the beginning of the sentence, the speaker will put a vocal stress at the end of the sentence to introduce a question.

آیا برف بارید؟
`ay`a barf b`ar`id?
Did it snow?

آیا مادر خود را دیدی؟
`ay`a m`adar-e khud r`a d`id`i?
Did you see your mother?

آیا کتابخانه رفتی؟
`ay`a kit`abkh`ana rafti?
Did you go to the library?

آیا کتاب را خریدی؟
`ay`a kit`ab r`a kharid`i?
Did you buy the book?

آیا خانه رفتی؟
`ay`a kh`ana rafti?
Did you go home?

In colloquial Dari, drop آیا *ay`a* from the beginning of the sentence and add a vocal stress at the end of the sentence.

برف بارید؟
barf b`ar`id?
Did it snow?

مادر خود را دیدی؟
m`adar-e khud r`a d`id`i?
Did you see your mother?

کتابخانه رفتی؟
kit`abkh`ana rafti?
Did you go to the library?

کتاب را خریدی؟
kit`ab r`a kharid`i?
Did you buy the book?

خانه رفتی؟
kh`ana rafti?
Did you go home?

تمرین Exercise

Dari sentences changed to questions. Write the Dari sentences as you read them.

شیلا خانه رفت.
Sheila kh`ana raft.
Sheila went home.

شیلا خانه رفت؟
Sheila kh`ana raft?
Did Sheila go home?

or

آیا شیلا خانه رفت؟
`ay`a Sheila kh`ana raft?
Did Sheila go home?

کاکا شما یک موتر خرید.
k`ak`a-e shom`a yak motar kharid.
Your uncle bought a car.

کاکا شما یک موتر خرید؟
k`ak`a-e shom`a yak motar kharid?
Did your uncle buy a car?

or

آیا کاکا شما یک موتر خرید؟
`ay`a k`ak`a-e shom`a yak motar kharid?
Did your uncle buy a car?

مادر او مریض است.
m`ader-e o mar`iz ast.
His mother is sick.

مادر او مریض است؟		آیا مادر او مریض است؟
m`ader-e o mar`iz ast?	**or**	*`ay`a m`ader-e o mar`iz ast?*
Is his mother sick?		Is his mother sick?

او مریض است.
o mar`iz ast.
She is sick.

او مریض است؟		آیا او مریض است؟
o mar`iz ast?	**or**	*`ay`a o mar`iz ast?*
Is she sick?		Is she sick?

باغ او کلان است.
b`agh-e o kal`an ast.
His garden is large.

باغ او کلان است		آیا باغ او کلان است؟
b`agh-e o kal`an ast?	**or**	*`ay`a b`agh-e o kal`an ast?*
Is his garden large?		Is his garden large?

صوفیا پنیر و تربوز از دکان خرید.
Sophia panir va tarb`uz az dok`an kharid.
Sophia bought cheese and watermelon from the store.

صوفیا پنیر و تربوز از دکان خرید؟
Sophia panir va tarb`uz az dok`an kharid?
Did Sophia buy cheese and watermelon from the store?

or

آیا صوفیا پنیر و تربوز از دکان خرید؟
`ay`a Sophia panir va tarb`uz az dok`an kharid?
Did Sophia buy cheese and watermelon from the store?

Vocabulary

خر	*khar*	donkey
نجار	*naj`ar*	carpenter
چارپائی	*ch`arp`aey*	bed (made from ropes)
پیر	*pir*	old, aged
جمعه	*juma*	Friday
دکان	*dok`an*	store
تربوز	*tarb`uz*	watermelon
پنیر	*panir*	cheese
کلان	*kal`an*	big, large
مریض	*mar`iz*	sick
دیدن	*d`idan*	to see
باریدن	*b`ar`idan*	to rain or to snow

Lesson Fifteen درس پانزدهم

Plural

In Dari ها *h`a,* ان *`an,* ات *at,* یل *el,* گان *g`an,* or یان *y`an* are used as suffixes to make nouns plural. Most nouns will become plural by adding ها *h`a* as a suffix. Some nouns will also become plural by adding ان *`an* as a suffix. In addition, a few nouns will become plural by adding ات *at* or یل *el* گان *g`an* or یان *y`an* as suffixes. Usually adding یل *el* will also change the form of the noun.

As a general rule, animate nouns such as people and animals will become plural by adding the suffix ان *`an* to their singular forms. A large number of animate nouns can become plural by adding either ان *`an* or ها *h`a* as suffixes. Adding the suffix ان *`an* is the correct form to make animate nouns plural. In many instances ها *h`a* is used instead of ان *`an* for animate nouns, which is also acceptable in Dari.

Some nouns become plural by adding the suffix ان *`an* or the suffix ها *h`a,* as shown in the following animate nouns. In many cases it is acceptable in Dari to use either ان *`an* or ها *h`a.*

مرد	*mard*	man
مردان	*mard`an*	men
مرد ها	*mard h`a*	men
زن	*zan*	woman
زنان	*zan`an*	women
زن ها	*zan h`a*	women

مرغ	*murgh*	chicken
مرغان	*murgh`an*	chickens
مرغ ها	*murgh h`a*	chickens

دختر	*dokhtar*	girl
دختران	*dokhtaran*	girls
دختر ها	*dokhtar h`a*	girls

A few animate nouns use گان *g`an* or یان *y`an*. When animate nouns end in ه *he*, the ending ه *he* is removed and گان *g`an* is added as a suffix. If ها *h`a* is used to make them plural the ه *he* will not be removed, the suffix ها *h`a* will be added after the ه *he*.

پرنده	*parenda*	bird
پرندگان	*parendag`an*	birds
پرنده ها	*parenda h`a*	birds

مورچه	*morcha*	ant
مورچگان	*morchag`an*	ants
مورچه ها	*morchah`a*	ants

When animate nouns end in ا *alef,* the suffix یان *y`an* is added to make them plural.

| آقا | *`aq`a* | gentleman |
| آقایان | *`aq`ay`an* | gentlemen |

Do not use the suffix ان *`an* with inanimate nouns under any circumstances. Inanimate nouns, like objects, use the suffix ها *h`a* only. The suffix ها *h`a* can be written jointly with the noun, or it can also be written separately after the noun.

Separately: چوکی ها *chawk`i h`a* (chairs), قلم ها *qalam h`a* (pens)
Jointly: چوکیها *chawk`ih`a* (chairs), قلمها *qalamh`a* (pens).

When the last letter of the noun ends in a non-connecting letter, the suffix ها *h`a* is always written separately as میزها *maiz h`a* (tables), دیوارها *diw`ar h`a* (walls), پرده ها *pardah h`a* (curtains), etc.

If a noun ends in ه *he*, the suffix ها will not be written jointly with the noun. It will be written separately like خانه ها *kh`ana h`a* (houses), دروازه ها *darw`aza h`a* (doors), تخته ها *takhta h`a* (boards), etc.

Inanimate nouns and their plural forms:

کتاب	*kit`ab*	book
کتابها or کتاب ها	*kit`abh`a*	books
قلم	*qalam*	pen
قلمها or قلم ها	*qalamh`a*	pens
خانه	*kh`ana*	house
خانه ها	*kh`anah`a*	houses

As the result of Arabic influence on the Dari language, some Arabic nouns are used in Dari. These nouns become plural by adding ات *at* or یل *el* as suffixes (same as Arabic), as well as by adding ها *h`a* (same as Dari). When یل *el* is added the form of the noun will change. Although the Arabic formats are acceptable in Dari, some of these nouns can also become plural by adding ها *h`a* as suffix.

رباعی	*rub`a'i*	quatrain
رباعیات	*rub`a'iat*	quatrains
رباعی ها	*rub`aay h`a*	quatrains
مسئله	*mas'ala*	question, problem
مسایل	*mas`ael*	questions, problems
مسئله ها	*mas'ala h`a*	questions, problems
قبیله	*qabila*	tribe
قبایل	*qabila*	tribes
قبیله ها	*qabila h`a*	tribes

General rules for pluralization of Dari nouns are:

- Most animate nouns can become plural by adding either ها *h`a* or ان *`an* as a suffix.
- All inanimate nouns become plural by adding the suffix ها *h`a*
- The suffix ان *`an* is attached to the noun when a noun ends with a connecting letter.
- The suffix ها *h`a* is written either jointly or separately after a noun.
- When a noun ends in ه *he*, the suffix ها *h`a* will not be connected to the noun it represents. It will always be written separately after the noun.

تمرین Exercise

Read as you write the following Dari nouns and their plural forms. These nouns can become plural by adding the suffix ها or adding the suffix ان. Few of the following nouns will use both ها and ان. Both forms are shown when nouns may become plural by adding both ها and ان.

چوب	چوب ها	خران
خر	خرها	
جگ	جگ ها	
شتر	شترها	شتران
رابر	رابرها	
برادر	برادر ها	برادران
مرد	مرد ها	مردان
پرده	پرده ها	
بز	بزها	بزان
نقشه	نقشه ها	
معلم	معلم ها	معلمان
مورچه	مورچه ها	مورچگان

Vocabulary

اسپ	*asp*	horse
باغ	*b`agh*	garden
چوب	*chub*	wood
جگ	*jug*	pitcher
شتر	*shutur*	camel
رابر	*r`abar*	rubber
پرده	*parda*	curtain
بز	*buz*	goat
مکتوب	*makt`ub*	letter
خانه	*kh`ana*	house
مورچه	*morcha*	ant
یک	*yak*	one, a
است	*ast*	is
پرنده	*parenda*	bird
آقا	*`aq`a*	gentleman, Mr.
آقایان	*`aq`ay`an*	gentlemen
میز	*maiz*	table
پرده	*pardah*	curtain
دیوار	*diw`ar*	wall
تخته	*takhta*	board
رباعی	*rub`a'i*	quatrain
مسئله	*mas`ala*	question, problem
قبیله	*qabila*	tribe

Lesson Sixteen درس شانزدهم

Suffixes ک k and چه cha

In Dari the suffix ک k is added to a noun for two reasons. One reason is an expression of love and respect and the second reason is to insult and degrade. Usually when suffix ک k is attached to children and family member, it is an expression of love and respect.

| دختر | dokhtar | girl |
| دخترک | dokhtarak | girl (the suffix ک k is a sign of love) |

| مادر | m`adar | mother |
| مادرک | madarak | mother (the suffix ک k is a sign of respect and love) |

| مرد | mard | man |
| مردک | mardak | man (the suffix ک k is to degrade the man) |

| نجار | naj`ar | carpenter |
| نجارک | naj`arak | carpenter (the suffix ک k is to degrade the carpenter) |

The suffix چه cha indicates a smaller value.

| باغ | b`agh | garden |
| باغچه | baghcha | small garden |

| صندوق | sand`uq | box |
| صندوقچه | sand`uqcha | small box |

تمرین Exercise

Write the following Dari sentences. Pronounce as you write.

دخترک همسایه مقبول است.

dokhtarak-e hams`aya maqbool ast.

The neighbor's girl is pretty.

معلم من یک باغچه خورد دارد.

mu'alim-e man yak baghcha-e khord d`arad.

My teacher has a small garden.

خواهرک من مکتب رفت.

khw`aharak-e man maktab raft.

My sister went to school.

مادر من یک صندوقچه سبز دارد.

m`ader-e man yak sand`uqcha-e sabz d`arad.

My mother has a small green box.

Vocabulary

خورد	*khord*	small
صندوق	*sand`uq*	box
صندوقچه	*sand`uqcha*	a small box
داشتن	*d`ashtan*	to have
دارد	*d`arad*	has (he, she, or it)
سبز	*sabz*	green

Part III

Grammar

Lesson Seventeen درس هفدهم

Personal Pronouns

A pronoun is a word that can replace a noun in a sentence. For example instead of saying, "John came," we can say, "he came." In this sentence, "he" is a personal pronoun.

Dari has no gender distinction. As we see below the third person in Dari is او *o*, used for he, she, or it.

First person:		
man	I	من
m`a	we	ما
	Second person:	
tu	you	تو
shom`a	you	شما
	Third person:	
o	he, she, or it	او
`anh`a	they	آنها

I	*man*	من
you	*tu* or *shom`a*	تو or شما
he	*o*	او
she	*o*	او
we	*m`a*	ما
they	*`anh`a*	آنها

تو *tu* and شما *shom`a*

تو *tu* is used for singular and شما *shom`a* is used for both plural and singular. تو *tu* does not have a plural form. تو *tu* is mostly used when speaking to close friends or children. شما *shom`a* is the polite form of تو *tu* and is used for respected and older individuals, strangers, and superiors. شما *shom`a* can be used for one person or for more than one person, depending on the context. تو *tu* is used in informal conversation and شما *shom`a* is used in formal conversation.

کتاب من	*kit`ab-e man*	my book
کتاب شما or کتاب تو	*kit`ab-e shom`a* or *kitab-e tu*	your book
کتاب او	*kit`ab-e o*	his book
کتاب او	*kitab-e o*	her book
کتاب ما	*kit`ab-e m`a*	our book
کتاب آنها	*kit`ab-e `anh`a*	their book
کتاب سبز من	*kit`ab-e sabz-e man*	my green book
کتاب سبز تو	*kit`ab-e sabz-e tu*	your green book
کتاب سبز او	*kit`ab-e sabz-e o*	his/her green book
کتاب سبز ما	*kit`ab-e sabz-e m`a*	our green book
کتاب سبز آنها	*kit`ab-e sabz-e `anh`a*	their green book

In colloquial Dari in Afghanistan, the word *man* من is changed to *ma* مه and the word *`anh`a* آنها is changed to *`un`a* اونا.

تمرین Exercise

Write the following Dari phrases. Read as you write.

باغ سبز من	*b`agh-e sabz-e man*	my green garden
باغ سبز تو	*b`agh-e sabz-e tu*	your green garden (for singular)
باغ سبز او	*b`agh-e sabz-e o*	his/her green garden
باغ سبز ما	*b`agh-e sabz-e m`a*	our green garden
باغ سبز شما	*b`agh-e sabz-e shom`a*	your green gardens (for plural)
باغ سبز آنها	*b`agh-e sabz-e `anh`a*	their green garden

Write the following Dari sentences. Read as you write.

آنها به مکتب رفتند.
`anh`a beh maktab raftand.
They went to school.

تو کجا رفتی؟
tu koj`a rafti?
Where did you go?

ما یک نقشه خریدیم.
m`a yak naqshah kharidim.
We bought a map.

من یک قلم سبز دارم.
man yak qalam-e sabz d`aram.
I have a green pen.

کتاب شما بالا میز است.
kit`ab-e shom`a b`ala-e maiz ast.
Your book is on the table.

Vocabulary

من	*man*	I
تو	*tu*	you
او	*o*	he/she
ما	*m`a*	we
شما	*shom`a*	you
آنها	*`anh`a*	they
ایشان	*aysh`an*	they

Lesson Eighteen درس هژدهم

Possessive Personal Pronoun Endings

Possessive personal pronouns in Dari have the following suffixes or endings and can be added to nouns, adjectives, and verbs.

	Singular		**Plural**	
1st person	م	*meem*	مان	*m`an*
2nd person	ت	*te*	تان	*t`an*
3rd person	ش	*sheen*	شان	*sh`an*

مادرم	*m`adaram*	my mother
مادرت	*m`adarat*	your mother
مادرش	*m`adarash*	his or her mother
مادرمان	*m`adar-em`an*	our mother
مادرتان	*m`adar-et`an*	your mother
مادر شان	*m`adar-esh`an*	their mother

دوستم	*dostam*	my friend
دوستت	*dostat*	your friend
دوستش	*dostash*	his or her friend
دوستمان	*dost-em`an*	our friend
دوستتان	*dost-et`an*	your friend
دوستشان	*dost-esh`an*	their friend

کتابم	*kit`abam*	my book
کتابت	*kit`abat*	your book
کتابش	*kit`abash*	his/her/ book
کتابمان	*kit`abem`an*	our book
کتابتان	*kit`abet`an*	your book
کتابشان	*kit`abesh`an*	their books

تمرین Exercise

Possessive personal endings added to the following words. Pronounce as you write in Dari. خواهر – پدر – برادر – اسپ

خوا هر *khw`ahar* (sister):

خواهرم	*khw`aharm*	my sister
خواهرت	*khw`ahart*	your sister
خواهرش	*khw`aharsh*	his/her sister
خواهرمان	*khw`ahar-e m`an*	our sister
خواهرتان	*khw`ahar-e t`an*	your sister
خواهرشان	*khw`ahar-e sh`an*	their sister

پدر *pedar* (father):

پدرم	*pedaram*	my father
پدرت	*pedarat*	your father
پدرش	*pedarash*	his/her father
پدرمان	*pedar-e m`an*	our father
پدرتان	*pedar-e t`an*	your father
پدرشان	*pedarash`an*	their father

برادر *ber`ader* (brother):

برادرم	*ber`aderam*	my brother
برادرت	*ber`aderat*	your brother
برادرش	*ber`aderash*	his/her brother
برادرمان	*ber`ader-e m`an*	our brother
برادرتان	*ber`ader-e t`an*	your brother
برادرشان	*ber`ader-e sh`an*	their brother

اسپ *asp* (horse):

اسپم	*aspam*	my horse
اسپت	*aspat*	your horse
اسپش	*aspash*	his/her horse
اسپمان	*asp-e m`an*	our horse
اسپتان	*asp-e t`an*	your horse
اسپشان	*asp-e sh`an*	their horse

Vocabulary

خواهر	*khw`ahar*	sister
کشتی	*kishti*	boat
دوست	*dost*	friend

Lesson Nineteen درس نزدهم

Use of Personal Endings with Plural Nouns

Personal endings are also used with plural nouns. For plural nouns that end in ها *h`a*, we add a ی *y* after the plural noun before adding the personal endings.

کتابهایم	*kit`abh`ayam*	my books
کتابهایت	*kit`abh`ayat*	your books
کتابهایش	*kit`abh`ayash*	his/her books
کتابهایمان	*kit`abh`a-em`an*	our books
کتابهایتان	*kit`abh`a-et`an*	your books
کتابهایشان	*kit`abh`a-esh`an*	their books
کشتی هایم	*kishtih`ayam*	my boats
کشتی هایت	*kishtih`ayat*	your boats
کشتی هایش	*kishtih`ayash*	his/her boats
کشتی هایمان	*kishtih`a-em`am*	our boats
کشتی هایتان	*kishih`a-et`an*	your boats
کشتی هایشان	*kishtih`a-esh`an*	their boats

We can write a personal ending separately after the noun as in کتاب هایم *kit`ab h`ayam*, کشتی هایم *kishtiy h`ayam*, or write it jointly attached to nouns as کتابهایم *kit`abh`ayam*, کشتیهایم *kishtiyh`ayam*. Both forms of writings to write ها *h`a* separately or jointly are acceptable in Dari.

Adding personal endings for plural nouns that do not end in ها *h`a* will not change the form of those nouns. For example, the plural of

اسپ *asp* (horse) is اسپان *asp ʿan* (horses). We add the personal endings to the plural form, as below:

اسپانم	*asp ʿanam*	my horses
اسپانت	*asp ʿanat*	your horses
اسپانش	*asp ʿanash*	his/her horses
اسپانمان	*asp ʿan-em ʿan*	our horses
اسپانتان	*asp ʿan-et ʿan*	your horses
اسپانشان	*asp ʿan-eshan*	their horses

تمرین Exercise

Possessive personal endings added to the following plural nouns. Pronounce as you write.

باغها – برادران – خواهران

باغ هایم	*b ʿagh h ʿayam*	my gardens
باغ هایت	*b ʿagh h ʿayat*	your gardens
باغ هایش	*b ʿagh h ʿayash*	his/her gardens
باغ هایمان	*b ʿagh h ʿa-em ʿan*	our gardens
باغ هایتان	*b ʿagh h ʿa-et ʿan*	your gardens
باغ هایشان	*b ʿagh h ʿa-esh ʿan*	their gardens
برادرانم	*ber ʿadar ʿanam*	my brothers
برادرانت	*ber ʿadar ʿanat*	your brothers
برادرانش	*ber ʿadar ʿanash*	his/her brothers
برادرانمان	*ber ʿadar ʿana-em ʿan*	our brothers
برادرانتان	*ber ʿadar ʿana-et ʿan*	your brothers
برادرانشان	*ber ʿadar ʿana-esh ʿan*	their brothers
خواهرانم	*khw ʿahar ʿanam*	my sisters
خواهرانت	*khw ʿahar ʿanat*	your sisters
خواهرانش	*khw ʿahar ʿanash*	his/her sisters
خواهرانمان	*khw ʿahar ʿan-em ʿan*	our sisters
خواهرانتان	*khw ʿahar ʿan-esh ʿan*	your sisters
خواهرانشان	*khw ʿahar ʿan-et ʿan*	their sisters

Vocabulary

خواهران	*khw`ahar`an*	sisters
پیاله	*pey`alah*	cup
شانه	*sh`anah*	comb; shoulder

Lesson Twenty درس بیستم

Adjectives

Adjectives describe the attributes of nouns. In Dari, adjectives usually follow nouns, and verbs will come last in a sentence. When a noun is singular or plural the adjective representing the noun will always remain singular. An added *ez`afa "-e"* sound will be added to the noun to qualify the adjective.

دختر خوب	*dokhtar-e kh`ub*	the good girl
دختران خوب	*dokhtar`an-e kh`ub*	the good girls
کتاب خورد	*ket`ab-e khord*	the small book
کتابها خورد	*ket`abh`a-e khord*	the small books
قلم سیاه	*qalam-e sey`a*	the black pen
قلمها سیاه	*qalamh`a-e sey`a*	the black pens

There are three degrees of adjectives in Dari. Absolute adjectives include خوب *kh`ub* (good), خورد *khord* (small), کلان *kal`an* (big), etc. Comparative adjectives include خوبتر *kh`ubtar* (better), خوبترین *kh`ubtar`in* (best); خوردتر *khordtar* (smaller), خوردترین *khordtar`in* (smallest); سیاه تر *sey`atar* (blacker), سیاه ترین *sey`atar`in* (blackest), etc. Suffix تر *tar,* and suffix ترین *tar`in* are added to the absolute forms of adjectives to constitute a comparison.

خوب	*kh`ub*	good
خوبتر	*kh`ubtar*	better
خوبترین	*kh`ubtarin*	best

کلان	kal`an	big
کلانتر	kal`antar	bigger
کلانترین	kal`antar`in	biggest
تاریک	t`ar`ik	dark
تاریکتر	t`ar`iktar	darker
تاریکترین	t`ar`iktar`in	darkest
گرم	garm	warm
گرمتر	garmtar	warmer
گرمترین	garmtar`in	warmest
خوشحال	khoshh`al	happy
خوشحالتر	khoshh`altar	happier
خوشحالترین	khoshh`altar`in	happiest
تنبل	tanbal	lazy
تنبل تر	tanbaltar	lazier
تنبل ترین	tanbaltar`in	laziest
سرد	sard	cold
سردتر	sardtar	colder
سردترین	sardtar`in	coldest
سفید	safed	white
سفیدتر	safedtar	whiter
سفیدترین	safedtar`in	whitest
دراز	dar`az	long
درازتر	dar`aztar	longer
درازترین	dar`aztar`in	longest

قلم سیاه از قلم سرخ کلانتر است.

qalam-e sey`a az qalam-e surkh kal`antar ast.

The black pen is bigger than the red pen.

کلانترین سیب را بگیر.

kal`antar`in seb r`a beg`ir.

Take the biggest apple.

این تاریکترین اطاق است.

i`n t`ar`iktar`in ut`aq ast.

This is the darkest room.

امروز گرمتر از دیروز است.

emruz garmtar az d`iruz ast.

Today is warmer than yesterday.

Vocabulary

سیب	seb	apple
بگیر	beg`ir	take
از	az	from
اطاق	ut`aq	room
در	dar	(preposition) in, into, within
خانه	kh`ana	house
روز	ruz	day
امروز	emruz	today
دیروز	d`iruz	yesterday
سفید	safed	white
شیرین	shireen	sweet
زرد	zard	yellow
تنبل	tanbal	lazy
مهربان	mehrab`an	kind
بلند	biland	tall, high
کوتاه	kot`ah	short
بزرگ	bozurg	big, large
دراز	dar`az	long
تاریک	t`ar`ik	dark
سرد	sard	cold
خوشحال	khoshh`al	happy
تر	tar	wet

Lesson Twenty-One درس بیست ویکم

Verbs: Infinitives

Verbs describe an action: you go, you are going, you do go; a process: you sleep, you are sleeping, you do sleep; or a state of being: it rains, it is raining, it does rain.

The Dari language does not make use of the passive voice when the active voice can be used. For example, we cannot say "The student was seen by Hasan." Instead, we say, "Hasan saw the student."

All infinitives of Dari verbs end in دن *dan* or تن *tan* or یدن *idan*.

خواندن	*khw'andan*	to read
دیدن	*didan*	to see
گرفتن	*gereftan*	to take
نوشتن	*navishtan*	to write
زدن	*zadan*	to hit
گفتن	*guftan*	to say
خوردن	*khordan*	to eat

The infinitive forms of verbs can be used as nouns.

خواندن خوب است	*khw'andan kh'ub ast*	reading is good.
دویدن آسان است	*dawidan 'as'an ast*	running is easy.
زدن خوب نیست	*zadan kh'ub neist*	hitting is not good.

تمرین Exercise

Write the following Dari sentences. Pronounce as you write in Dari.

خواندن آسان است

khw`andan `as`an ast

reading is easy

دست شستن خوب است

dast shustan kh`ub ast

washing hands is good

دویدن مشکل است

daw`idan mushkil ast

running is difficult

گریه کردن بد است

girya kardan bad ast

crying is bad

Vocabulary

خوردن	*khordan*	to eat
گفتن	*guftan*	to say
زدن	*zadan*	to hit
نوشتن	*navishtan*	to write
گرفتن	*gereftan*	to take
دیدن	*d`idan*	to see
خواندن	*khw`andan*	to read
گریه کردن	*girya kardan*	to cry
دست	*dast*	hand
مشکل	*mushkil*	difficult

Lesson Twenty-Two درس بیست و دوم

Present Tense

As mentioned earlier all infinitive forms of verbs end in دن *dan,* تن *tan,* or یدن *idan.* To form the present tense drop the دن *dan,* تن *tan,* or یدن *idan* from the infinitive forms of verb endings, add the present prefix می *may* to the verbs, then add personal endings.

Personal endings, as we saw earlier, are:

Singular		**Plural**	
1st person	م	1st person	یم
2nd person	ید	2nd person	ید
3rd person	(no ending)	3rd person	ند

For example, the infinitive form of the verb to eat is خوردن *khordan;* drop the دن *dan* then add the personal endings to خور *khor.* The personal ending for I is م *meem.* Add م *meem* for I and the present prefix می *may* to get the first person singular of to eat: می خورم *may khoram*

You can write as one word میخورم *maykhoram* or separately as می خورم *may khoram.* Both forms of writing are acceptable in Dari.

من میخورم	*man maykhoram*	I eat
تو میخوری	*tu maykhore*	You eat
او میخورد	*o maykhorad*	He/she eats
ما میخوریم	*m`a mayekhoraim*	We eat
شما میخورید	*shom`a maykhoraid*	You eat
آنها میخورند	*`anh`a maykhorand*	They eat

من سیب میخورم.	man seb maykhoram.	I eat apple.
تو سیب میخوری.	tu seb maykhore.	You eat apple.
او سیب میخورد.	o seb maykhorad.	He eats apple.
او سیب میخورد.	o seb maykhorad.	She eats apple.
این سیب میخورد.	i'n seb maykhorad.	It eats apple.
ما سیب میخوریم.	m'a seb maykhoraim.	We eat apple.
آنها سیب میخورند.	'anh'a seb maykhorand.	They eat apple.

When present stems end in ‌ا *alef,* add ی or ‌ن‌ *y* to the present stem before adding the personal endings. For example, the present stem of the verb آمدن ‌ *'amadan* (to come) is آ ‌`a. Add the present prefix می *may* to get می آ *may'a.* Since the present stem ends in ‌ا *alef,* we add a ی to it before adding the personal ending to get می آیم *may'aym.*

می *may* can be written separately as می آیم or jointly as میآیم. Both forms of writing are acceptable in Dari.

من میآیم	man may'aym	I come
تو میآئی	tu may'aye	You come
او میآید	o may'ayad	He comes
او میآید	o may'ayad	She comes
این میآید	i'n may'ayad	It comes
ما میآئیم	m'a may'ayaim	We come
آنها میآیند	'anh'a may'ayand	They come

All Dari verbs have regular past stems. However, the present stems of some Dari verbs are irregular.

Here are some examples of verbs that have regular present stems:

Infinitive			Present stem	
آوردن	'awardan	to bring	آور	'awar
خریدن	kharidan	to buy	خر	khar
خوردن	khordan	to eat	خور	khor
خواندن	khw'andan	to read	خوان	khw'an

And some examples of irregular present stems:

	Infinitive			Present stem	
بودن	*budan*	to be	هست	*hast*	
گرفتن	*gereftan*	to take	گیر	*gir*	
رفتن	*raftan*	to go	رو	*rav*	
دادن	*d`adan*	to give	ده	*deh*	
دیدن	*d`idan*	to see	بین	*b`in*	
نوشتن	*navishtan*	to write	نویس	*nav`is*	
گذشتن	*gozashtan*	to pass	گذر	*gozar*	
گفتن	*goftan*	to say	گو	*go*	
نشستن	*nishastan*	to sit	نشین	*nish`in*	

Exercise تمرین

The infinitive forms of the following verbs changed to present stems and then added personal endings. Pronounce as you write.

بودن   *budan* (to be)

من هستم	*man hastam*	I am
تو هستی	*tu hasti*	you are
او هست	*o hast*	he/she is
این هست	*`in hast*	this is
ما هستیم	*m`a hastaim*	we are
آنها هستند	*`anh`a hastand*	they are

آوردن   *`awardan* (to bring)

من می آورم	*man may `awaram*	I bring
تو می آوری	*tu may `awari*	you bring
او می آورد	*o may `awarad*	he/she brings
ما می آوریم	*m`a may `awaraim*	we bring
شما می آورید	*shom`a may `awaraid*	you bring
آنها می آورند	*`anh`a may `awarand*	they bring

خريدن *kharidan* (to buy)

من ميخرم	*man maykharam*	I buy
تو ميخری	*tu maykhari*	you buy
او ميخرد	*o maykharad*	he/she buys
ما ميخريم	*m`a maykharaim*	we buy
شما ميخريم	*shom`a maykharaid*	you buy
آنها ميخرند	*`anh`a maykharaim*	they buy

The following English sentences translated in Dari. Pronounce as you write the Dari sentences.

I am a student.	من يک شاگرد هستم.	*man yak sh`agird hastam.*
You are a student.	تو يک شاگرد هستی.	*tu yak sh`agird hasti.*
He is a student.	او يک شاگرد است.	*o yak sh`agird hast.*
She is a student.	او يک شاگرد است.	*o yak sh`agird hast.*
We are students.	ما شاگرد هستيم.	*m`a sh`agird hastim.*
They are students.	آنها شاگرد هستند.	*`anh`a sh`agird hastand.*

Vocabulary

آوردن	*awardan*	to bring
نشستن	*nishastan*	to sit
گفتن	*goftan*	to say
نوشتن	*navishtan*	to write
دادن	*d`adan*	to give
بودن	*budan*	to be
آمدن	*`amadan*	to come
سيب	*seb*	apple

Lesson Twenty-Three   درس بیست و سوم

Past Tense

Verbs have present and past stems that are the basis for various tenses. The past stem of verbs are formed by removing the ن *an* ending from the infinitive forms of the verbs. For example خواندن *khw`andan* (to read), دیدن *d`idan* (to see), گرفتن *gereftan* (to take), and نوشتن *navishtan* (to write) are the infinitive forms of verbs. When the ن *an* ending is removed, the infinitive forms of verbs change to past stem.

خواند	*khw`and*	read
دید	*d`id*	saw
گرفت	*gereft*	took
نوشت	*navisht*	wrote

To form the past tense we add the personal endings to the past stem, except for the third person singular, which has no ending.

As we saw earlier the personal endings are:

Singular		**Plural**	
1st person	م	1st person	یم
2nd person[7]	ید or ی	2nd person	ید
3rd person	(no ending)	3rd person	ند

The past stem of the verb خواندن *khw`andan* is خواند *khw`and*. To form the past tense we add the personal endings, while the past stem does not change.

---

[7] ی is used with تو *tu* and ید is used with *shom`a*.

Singular:

1st person	خواندم	*khw`andam*
2nd person	خواندی	*kw`andi*
3rd person	خواند	*khw`and*

Plural:

1st person	خواندیم	*khwandim*
2nd person	خواندید	*khw`andid*
3rd person	خواندند	*khw`andand*

من خواندم	*man khw`andam*	I read
تو خواندی	*tu kw`andi*	You read
او خواند	*o khw`and*	He/she/it
ما خواندیم	*m`a khwandim*	We read
شما خواندید	*shom`a khw`andid*	You read
آنها خواندند	*`anh`a khw`andand*	They read

من این کتاب [8]را خواندم.
man `in kit`ab r`a khw`andam.
I read this book.

تو این کتاب را خواندی.
t´u `in kit`ab r`a khw`and`i.
You read this book.

او این کتاب را خواند.
o `in kit`ab r`a khw`and.
He/she/it read this book.

ما این کتاب را خواندیم.
m`a `in kit`ab r`a khw`and`im.
We read this book.

شما این کتاب را خواندید.
shom`a `in kit`ab r`a khw`and`id.
You read this book.

آنها این کتاب را خواندند.
`anh`a `in kit`ab r`a khw`andand.
They read this book.

---

[8] See rule for the use of را *r`a*

The infinitive داشتن *d`ashtan* (to have) becomes داشت *d`asht* (had).

من داشتم	*man d`ashtam*	I had
تو داشتی	*tu d`ashti*	You had
او داشت	*o d`asht*	He had
او داشت	*o d`asht*	She had
این داشت	*`in d`ash*	It had
ما داشتیم	*ma d`ashtim*	We had
آنها داشتند	*`anh`a d`ashtand*	They had

The infinitive رفتن *raftan* (to go) becomes رفت *raft* (went).

من رفتم	*man raftam*	I went
تو رفتی	*tu rafti*	You went
او رفت	*o raft*	He went
او رفت	*o raft*	She went
این رفت	*`in raft*	It went
ما رفتیم	*m`a raft`im*	We went
شما رفتید	*shom`a raftaid*	You went
آنها رفتند	*`anh`a raftand*	They went

تمرین Exercise

Write the Dari sentences and pronounce as you write.

من مکتب رفتم.
man maktab raftam.
I went to school.

شیلا مکتب رفت.
Sheila maktab raft.
Sheila went to school.

شیلا کار خانگی خود را خلاص کرد.
Sheila k`ar-e kh`anagi khud r`a khal`as kard.
Sheila finished her homework.

کاکا من آمد.
k`ak`a-e man `amad.
My uncle came.

ما کتاب را خواندیم.
m`a kit`ab r`a khwandaim.
We read the book.

In Dari, verbs usually come at the end of sentences. In the following sentences we add time or a date to past tense sentences.

من این کتاب را خواندم.
man `in kit`ab r`a khw`andam
I read this book.

To add time or date as:

من دیروز این کتاب را خواندم.
man d`iruz `in kit`ab r`a khw`andam.
I read this book yesterday.

تو دیروز این کتاب را خواندی.
t`u d`iruz `in kit`ab r`a khw`andi.
You read this book yesterday.

او دیروز این کتاب را خواند.
o d`iruz `in kit`ab r`a khw`and.
He/she/it read this book yesterday.

ما دیروز این کتاب را خواندیم.
m`a d`iruz `in kit`ab r`a khw`and`im.
We read this book yesterday.

شما دیروز این کتاب را خواندید.
shom`a d`iruz `in kit`ab r`a khw`and`id.
You read this book yesterday.

آنها دیروز این کتاب را خواندند.
`anh`a d`iruz `in kit`ab r`a khw`andand.
They read this book yesterday.

من هفته گذشته به موزیم رفتم.
man hafta-e gozashtah beh muzium raftam.
I went to the museum last week.

تو هفته گذشته به موزیم رفتی.
tu hafta-e gozashtah beh muzium rafti.
You went to the museum last week.

او هفته گذشته به موزیم رفت.
o hafta-e gozashtah beh muzium raft.
He/she went to the museum last week.

ما هفته گذشته به موزیم رفتیم.
m`a hafta-e gozashtah beh muzium raftim.
We went to the museum last week.

آنها هفته گذشته به موزیم رفتند.
`anh`a hafta-e gozashtah beh muzium raftand.
They went to the museum last week.

Personal endings are also used when the subject is a proper noun as in the following sentences:

شیلا به کتابخانه رفت.
Sheil`a beh kit`abkh`ana raft.
Sheila went to the Library.

شیلا و محمود به کتابخانه رفتند.
Sheil`a va Mahm`ud beh kit`abkh`ana raftand.
Sheila and Mahmud went to the Library.

شیلا و من به کتابخانه رفتیم.
Sheil`a va man beh kit`abkh`ana raftaim.
Sheila and I went to the Library.

تمرین Exercise

Write the following Dari paragraph and read as you write.

شیلا هفته گذشته به دکان رفت۰ او یک قلم و یک پنسل خرید۰ او قلم
و پنسل را به مکتب برد۰ دوستان او قلمش را خوش کردند۰ دیروز شیلا
ساعت یک بجه از مکتب به خانه آمد۰ مادر و برادرش در خانه منتظرش
بودند۰ شیلا به همراه مادر و برادر خود به سینما رفت۰ آنها فلم را
خوش کردند۰

Translation:
Sheila went to the store last week. She bought a pen and a pencil. She
took the pen and the pencil to school. Her friends liked her pen. Yesterday she came home from school at one o'clock. Her mother and her
brother were waiting for her at home. Sheila went to the movie with her
mother and her brother. They liked the movie.

Vocabulary

بجه	*baja*	o'clock
یک	*yak*	one
آمدن	*`amadan*	to come
بریدن	*bur`idan*	to cut
کتابخانه	*kit`abkh`ana*	library
موزیم	*muzium*	museum
هفته	*hafta*	week
روز	*ruz*	day
امروز	*emruz*	today
دیروز	*d`iruz*	yesterday
بازی	*b`azi*	play
بازی کردن	*b`azi kardan*	to play
پنسل	*pensil*	pencil
گذشته	*gozashta*	last, past
دوست	*dost*	friend
خلاص کردن	*khal`as kardan*	to finish
کار خانگی	*k`ar-e kh`anagi*	homework
خوش داشتن	*khosh d`ashtan*	to like

Lesson Twenty-Four درس بیست و چهارم

Future Tense

The future tense is expressed in Dari by adding the word *khw`ahad* خواهد meaning "will" as a prefix to the personal ending. It comes before the verb. In daily conversation in Afghanistan *khw`ahad* is pronounced *kh`ad*.

داشتن   *d`ashtan*   (to have):

من خواهد داشتم	*man khw`ah d`ashtam*	I will have
تو خواهد داشتی	*tu khw`ahad d`ashti*	You will have
او خواهد داشت	*o khw`ahad d`asht*	He will have
او خواهد داشت	*o khw`ahad d`asht*	She will have
این خواهد داشت	*`in khw`ahad d`asht*	It will have
ما خواهد داشتیم	*m`a khw`ahad d`ashtim*	We will have
شما خواهد داشتید	*shom`a khw`ahad d`ashtid*	You[9] will have
آنها خواهد داشتند	*`anh`a khw`ahad d`ashtand*	They will have

خواندن *khw`andan* (to read):

من مکتوب را خواهد خواندم.
man makt`ub r`a khw`aham khw`andam.
I will read the letter.

تو مکتوب را خواهد خواندی.
tu makt`ub r`a khw`ahad khw`andi.
You will read the letter.

---

[9] For plural

او مکتوب را خواهد خواند.

o makt`ub r`a khw`ahad khw`and.

He will read the letter.

او مکتوب را خواهد خواند.

o makt`ub r`a khw`ahad khw`and.

She will read the letter.

این مکتوب را خواهد خواند.

`in makt`ub r`a khw`ahad khw`and.

It will read the letter.

شما مکتوب را خواهد خواندید.

shoma makt`ub r`a khw`ahad khw`andid.

You will read the letter.

ما مکتوب را خواهدخواندیم.

m`a makt`ub r`a khw`ahad khw`andim.

We will read the letter.

آنها مکتوب را خواهد خواندند.

`anh`a makt`ub r`a khw`ahad khw`andand.

They will read the letter.

Personal endings added to خواهد خورد (will eat) and
خواهد گرفت (will take):

من خواهد خوردم.	*man khw`ahad khordam.*	I will eat.
تو خواهد خوردی.	*tu khw`ahad khordi.*	You will eat.
او خواهد خورد.	*o khw`ahad khord.*	He/she eat.
ما خواهد خوردیم.	*m`a khw`ahad khordaim.*	We will eat.
شما خواهد خوردید.	*shom`a khw`ahad khordid.*	You will eat.
آنها خواهد خوردند.	*`anh`a khw`ahad khordand.*	They will eat.
من خواهد گرفتم.	*man khw`ahad griftam.*	I will take.
تو خواهد گرفتی.	*tu khw`ahad grifti.*	You will take.
او خواهد گرفت.	*o khw`ahad grift.*	He/She will take.
ما خواهد گرفتیم.	*m`a khw`ahad griftaim.*	We will take.
شما خواهد گرفتید.	*shom`a khw`ahad griftaid.*	You will take.
آنها خواهد گرفتند.	*`anh`a khw`ahad griftand.*	They will take.

تمرین Exercise

Read as you write the following Dari paragraph.

شیلا خواهر حسن است. آنها سال آینده یک خانه کلان خواهد خریدند. شیلا در کارته چهار زندگی میکند و حسن در خیر خانه زندگی میکند. سال آینده هر دو شان در یک خانه زندگی خواهد کردند.

Translation:
Sheila is Hasan's sister. Next year they will buy a big house. Sheila lives in Kart-e Char and Hasan lives in Khair Khana. Next year both of them will live in one house.

Vocabulary

زندگی	*zindagi*	life
زندگی کردن	*zindagi kardan*	to live
کارته چهار	*K`art-e Ch`ar*	name of a district in Kabul
خریدن	*kharidan*	to buy
کلان	*kal`an*	big, large
سال	*s`al*	year
سال آینده	*s`al-e `ayenda*	next year
هر دو شان	*har du-e sh`an*	both of them
خیرخانه	*Khir Kh`ana*	name of a district in Kabul

Lesson Twenty-Five درس بیست و پنجم

Negative Verbs

All verbs, irrespective of their tense, are made negative by adding the ن *na* prefix to them. Like شما خوردید *shom`a khord`id* (you ate), to make it negative we add the prefix نـ *na* to the verb خوردید *khord`id* to become شما نخوردید *shom`a nakhord`id* (you did not eat).

When a verb begins with a vowel, we add نیـ instead of نـ as the prefix. Such as شما آمدید *shom`a `amad`id* (you came). To make it negative attach the نیـ to the verb as: شما نیآمدید *shom`a nay`amad`id* (you did not come).

Sometimes double negatives are used in Dari. The Dari word هیچ *haich,* which means at all, or nothing, is added to a negative statement and it is called a double negative like:

هیچ نخوردم	*haich nakhordam*	did not eat [at all]
هیچ ندیدم	*haich nad`idam*	did not see [at all]

The following are positive and negative sentences:

من هر روز سیب میخورم.
man har ruz seb maykhoram.
I eat apple every day.

من هر روز سیب نمیخورم.
man har ruz seb namaykhoram.
I do not eat apple every day.

من هفته چهل ساعت کار میکنم.
man hafta-e chehil s`a'at k`ar maykonam.
I work forty hours a week.

من هفته چهل ساعت کار نمیکنم.
man hafta-e chehil s`a'at k`ar namaykonam.
I do not work forty hours a week.

او کتاب خود را در صبح میخواند.
o kit`ab-e khod r`a dar sobh maykhw`anad.
She reads her book in the morning.

او کتاب خود را در صبح نمیخواند.
o kit`ab-e khod r`a dar sobh namaykhw`anad.
She does not read her book in the morning.

Double Negatives

The double negative is not used in English. However, it is used in Dari. The exact translation of Dari double negative sentences as shown below are not correct English sentences. The translation is done to show the use of double negatives in Dari.

من هیچ مکتب نرفتم.
man haich maktab naraftam.
I did not go to school, [at all].

او هیچ نخورد.
o haich nakhord.
He did not eat, [at all].

ما هیچ ندیدیم.
m`a haich nadidim.
We nothing did not see.

If we remove the word هیچ *haich* (nothing or at all) from the negative Dari sentence it will still be a correct sentence in Dari.

من مکتب نرفتم.	*man maktab naraftam.*	I did not go to school.
او نخورد.	*o nakhord.*	He did not eat.
ما ندیدیم.	*m`a nadidim.*	We did not see.

تمرین Exercise

The following positive sentences are first changed to negative, and then to double negative sentences. Pronounce as you write.

شیلا مکتب رفت.
Sheila maktab raft.
Sheila went to school.

شیلا مکتب نرفت.
Sheila maktab naraft.
Sheila did not go to school.

شیلا هیچ مکتب نرفت.
Sheila haich maktab raraft.
Sheila did not go to school, [at all.]

_____

او معلم است.
o mu'alim ast.
He is a teacher.

او معلم نیست.
o mu'alim neast.
He is not a teacher.

او هیچ معلم نیست.
o haich mu'alim neast.
He is not a teacher, [at all.]

_____

پدر من دکاندار است.
pedar-e man dok`and`ar ast.
My father is a shopkeeper.

پدر من دکاندار نیست.
pedar-e man dok`and`ar neast.
My father is not a shopkeeper.

پدر من هیچ دکاندار نیست.
pedar-e man haich dok`and`ar neast.
My father is not a shopkeeper, [at all.]

_____

من هر روز دری میخوانم.
man har ruz Dari maykhw`anam.
I read Dari every day.

من هر روز دری نمیخوانم.
man har ruz Dari namaykhw`anam.
I do not read Dari everyday.

من هر روز هیچ دری نمیخوانم.
man har ruz haich Dari namaykhw`anam.
I do not read Dari everyday, [at all.]

من دو خواهر دارم.
man du khw`ahar d`aram.
I have two sisters.

من دو خواهر ندارم.
man du khw`ahar nad`aram.
I do not have two sisters.

من هیچ دو خواهر ندارم.
man haich du khw`ahar nad`aram.
I do not have two sisters, [at all.]

من همسایه خود را دیدم.
man hams`aya-e khud r`a d`idam.
I saw my neighbor.

من همسایه خود را ندیدم.
man hams`aya-e khud r`a nad`idam.
I did not see my neighbor.

من هیچ همسایه خود را ندیدم.
man haich hams`aya-e khud r`a nad`idam.
I did not see my neighbor, [at all.]

Vocabulary

دو ساله	du s`ala	two years old
بوت	boot	shoes
دفتر	daftar	office
دکان	dok`an	shop
دکاندار	dok`andar	shopkeeper
صبح	sobh	morning
ساعت	s`a'at	hour
چهل	chehil	forty
هیچ	haich	nothing, at all
هر روز	har ruz	everyday
پایتخت	p`aitakht	capital

Lesson Twenty-Six درس بیست و ششم

Prepositions

There are two types of Dari prepositions. One type of preposition requires *ez'afa* when they join with the noun that they modify, while the other type does not.

Dari prepositions without *ez'afa* include: از[10] *az* (than, from), با *b'a* (with), به *beh* (to, with), بی *be* (without), تا *t'a* (as far as, by the time, until), جز *joz* (except), در *dar* (in), and بر *bar* (on). The letter به *be* is used as a preposition prefix, and it would mean "to," as in English.

من	*man*	me
بمن	*beman*	to me
شما	*shoma*	you
بشما	*beshoma*	to you
او	*o*	he/she
به او	*beh o*	to him / to her
این	*'in*	it
به این	*beh 'in*	to it
ما	*m'a*	us
بما	*bem'a*	to us
آنها	*'anh'a*	them
به آنها	*beh 'anh'a*	to them

---

[10] از is also used for comparison. For example, کلانتر از means bigger than.

When a word begins with a long ﺍ *alef* or with a short ﺍ *alef*, the ﺑ *be* prefix can be written attached to the word, or it can also be written separately. When it is written separate from the word, a ﻩ *he* is added at the end of ﺑ *be* as ﺑﻪ *beh*. For example as in: ﺑﻪ ﺍﻳﻦ، ﺑﻪ ﺍﻭ، ﺑﻪ ﺁﻧﻬﺎ

ﺍﻭ ﺍﺧﺒﺎﺭ ﺭﺍ ﺑﻤﻦ ﺩﺍﺩ.
o akhb`ar r`a beman d`ad.
He gave the newspaper to me.

ﺍﻭ ﭘﻴﺴﻪ ﺭﺍ ﺑﻤﺎ ﺩﺍﺩ.
o paisa r`a bem`a d`ad.
He gave the money to us.

ﺍﻭ ﻗﺼﻪ ﺧﻮﺩ ﺭﺍ ﺑﻪ ﺁﻧﻬﺎ ﮔﻔﺖ.
o qisa-e khod r`a beh `anh`a goft.
He told his story to them.

Prepositions that join the noun with an *ez`afa* include: ﻃﺮﻑ *taraf* (towards, in the direction of), ﺩﺍﺧﻞ *d`akhil* (inside), ﺑﺪﻭﻥ *bed`un* (without), and ﺩﺭﺑﺎﺭﻩ *darb`arah* (about).

without him	*bed`un-e o*	ﺑﺪﻭﻥ ﺍﻭ
next to the door	*pahlu-e darw`aza*	ﭘﻬﻠﻮ ﺩﺭﻭﺍﺯﻩ
under the carpet	*zir-e q`alin*	ﺯﻳﺮ ﻗﺎﻟﻴﻦ

تمرین   Exercise

Write the Dari text. Pronounce as you write.

شیلا و من در دفتر باهم کار میکنیم · شیلا هر روز سه ساعت بالا
کمپیوتر کار میکند و دو ساعت در کتابخانه عامه کابل · ما هر روز در
حدود ده دقیقه پیاده میرویم و بعد سرویس میگیریم · خانه شیلا پهلو
خانه من است · ما اکثر وقت با هم هستیم ·

Translation:
Sheila and I work together in the office. Sheila works three hours every
day on computer, and two hours at the Kabul Public Library. We walk
for about ten minutes, and then we take a bus. Sheila's house is next to
my house. We spend most of our time together.

Vocabulary

طرف	*taraf*	towards, in the direction of
پیسه	*paisa*	money
خبر	*khabar*	news
اخبار	*akhb`ar*	newspaper
بر	*bar*	on
در	*dar*	in
جز	*joz*	except
بدون	*bed`un*	without
به	*beh*	to, with
با	*b`a*	with
از	*az*	than, from
پهلو	*pahlu*	next to
درباره	*darb`arah*	about
داخل	*d`akhil*	inside, in
باهم	*b`aham*	together
اکثر	*aksar*	often

Part IV

Vocabulary

Lesson Twenty-Seven درس بیست و هفتم

Numbers

Dari uses the Arabic numeral system as shown below. Dari numbers are written the same as in English. For example, you can write one hundred forty-nine as: ۱۴۹. You write from left to right, first 1, then 4, and then 9. See following examples.

۲۱۵۰	*du haz`aro yak sado pinj`ah*	2150
۴۵۰	*chah`ar sado pinj`ah*	450
۲۵۹۶	*du haz`aro panj sado navado shesh*	2596
۱۲	*duv`azdah*	12
۶۴۴	*shesh sado chehilo chah`ar*	644

Ordinal Numbers

first	*avval*	اول
second	*duvum*	دوم
third	*sehum*	سوم
fourth	*chaharum*	چهارم
fifth	*panjum*	پنجم
sixth	*seshum*	ششم
seventh	*haftum*	هفتم
eighth	*astum*	هشتم
ninth	*nuhum*	نهم
tenth	*dahum*	دهم

Cardinal Numbers (Words and Symbols)

zero	*sefer*	صفر	۰
one	*yak*	یک	۱
two	*du*	دو	۲
three	*se*	سه	۳
four	*chah`ar*	چهار	۴
five	*panj*	پنج	۵
six	*shesh*	شش	۶
seven	*haft*	هفت	۷
eight	*hasht*	هشت	۸
nine	*nuh*	نه	۹
ten	*dah*	ده	۱۰
eleven	*y`azdah*	یازده	۱۱
twelve	*duv`azdah*	دوازده	۱۲
thirteen	*sezdah*	سیزده	۱۳
fourteen	*chah`ardah*	چهارده	۱۴
fifteen	*p`anzdah*	پانزده	۱۵
sixteen	*sh`anzdah*	شانزده	۱۶
seventeen	*haftdah*	هفتده	۱۷
eighteen	*hazhdah*	هژده	۱۸
nineteen	*nuzdah*	نزده	۱۹
twenty	*b`ist*	بیست	۲۰
thirty	*see*	سی	۳۰
forty	*chehil*	چهل	۴۰
fifty	*pinj`ah*	پنجاه	۵۰
sixty	*shast*	شصت	۶۰
seventy	*haft`ad*	هفتاد	۷۰
eighty	*hasht`ad*	هشتاد	۸۰
ninety	*navad*	نود	۹۰
hundred	*sad*	صد	۱۰۰
thousand	*haz`ar*	هزار	۱۰۰۰

Mathematical Symbols

minus	*manfi*	منفی
plus	*jama'*	جمع
equal	*mas`awi*	مساوی
divided	*taqs`im*	تقسیم
percent	*f`isad*	فیصد

Examples:

شیلا ۵ [11]دانه سیب خرید.
Sheila panj d`ana seb kharid.
Sheila bought five apples.

شیلا ۳ دانه چوکی آورد.
Sheila se d`ana chawk`i `award.
Sheila brought three chairs.

او ۲۵۰ افغانی دارد.
o du sado pinj`ah Afgh`ani d`arad.
He has two hundred fifty Afghanis.

مکتب ۴۴۹۶ شاگرد دارد.
maktab chah`ar haz`aro chah`ar sado navado shesh sh`agird d`arad.
The school has four thousand four hundred ninety six students.

---

[11]Unit that is used between numerals and countable nouns.

تمرین Exercise

Write the following Dari numbers, and pronounce as you write.

۱۱۹۵	*yak haz`aro yak sado navado panj*	1195
۲۱۰	*du sado dah*	210
۱۰۵۹	*yak haz`aro pinj`aho nuh*	1059
۳۳۸۸	*se haz`aro se sado hasht`ado hasht*	3388
۲۱۷۸	*du haz`aro yak sado haft`ado hasht*	2178
۴۵۹۸۰	*chehilo panj haz`aro nuh sado hashtad*	45980

Write the following Dari text and numbers. Pronounce as you write.

من ۵۰۰ افغانی در بانک دارم.
man panj sad Afghani dar b`ank d`aram.
I have 500 Afghanis in the bank.

من چهار هزار و پنجصد و پنجاه و پنج کتاب دارم.
man chah`ar haz`aro panj sado pinj`aho panj kit`ab d`aram.
I have four thousand five hundred fifty-five books.

او دو صد و سی و هشت شاگرد دارد.
o du sado seeo hasht sh`agird d`arad.
She has two hundred thirty eight students.

شیلا در صنف چهارم است.
Sheila dar sinf-e chah`arum ast.
Sheila is in fourth grade.

من سی و هشت افغانی برای تکسی کار دارم.
man seeo hasht Afgh`ani bar`aye taksi k`ar d`aram.
I need thirty eight Afghani for the taxi.

من چاپ اول کتاب دری را کار دارم.
man ch`ap-e avval-e kit`ab-e Dari r`a k`ar d`aram.
I need the first edition of the Dari book.

Vocabulary

صفر	*sefer*	zero
سه	*seh*	three
پنج	*panj*	five
شش	*shesh*	six
هفت	*haft*	seven
هشت	*hasht*	eight
نه	*nuh*	nine
ده	*dah*	ten
بیست	*b`ist*	twenty
سی	*see*	thirty
چهل	*chehil*	forty
پنجاه	*pinj`ah*	fifty
شصت	*shast*	sixty
هفتاد	*haft`ad*	seventy
هشتاد	*hasht`ad*	eighty
نود	*navad*	ninety
صد	*sad*	hundred
هزار	*haz`ar*	thousand
ملیون	*million*	million
منفی	*manfi*	minus
جمع	*jama'*	plus
مساوی	*mas`awi*	equal
تقسیم	*taqs`im*	divided by
فیصد	*fisad*	percent
چاپ	*ch`ap*	edition

Lesson Twenty-Eight درس بیست و هشتم

Days and Months

Days of the Week

In Afghanistan, government offices are open Saturday through Thursday. Saturday is the first working day of the week. The normal workday is from 8:00 a.m. to 5:00 p.m. On Thursdays, some offices close at noon. Friday is the weekend and all official businesses are closed.

شنبه	*shanbe*	Saturday
یکشنبه	*yak shanbe*	Sunday
دوشنبه	*du shanbe*	Monday
سه شنبه	*seh shanbe*	Tuesday
چهارشنبه	*chah`ar shanbe*	Wednesday
پنجشنبه	*panj shanbe*	Thursday
جمعه	*juma'*	Friday

تمرین Exercise

Read and write the following Dari paragraph.

شیلا در وزارت معارف کار میکند. او هر روز ساعت هفت صبح خانه را
ترک میکند و به ایستگاه سرویس میرود. شیلا به ساعت هشت به کار
خود شروع میکند. او هفته پنج روز در دفتر کار میکند. روز ها
پنجشنبه و روز ها جمعه شیلا در خانه است.

Translation:
Sheila works at the Ministry of Education. Every morning she leaves
home at seven o'clock and goes to the bus stop. Sheila starts her work
at eight o'clock. She works five day a week in her office. Sheila is at
home on Thursdays and Fridays.

Write the following Dari sentences. Pronounce as you write.

در افغانستان شنبه روز اول هفته است ·
dar Afgh`anist`an shanbe ruz-e avval-e hafta ast.
In Afghanistan Saturday is the first day of the week.

من روز ها جمعه به خانه خواهرم میروم ·
man ruz h`aye juma' beh kh`ana-e khw`aharam mayrawam.
On Fridays I go to my sister's house.

صوفیا دیروز مکتب نرفت ·
Sophia d`iruz maktab naraft.
Sophia did not go to school yesterday.

کتابخانه عامه از ساعت هفت صبح تا شش شام باز است ·
kit`ab kh`ana-e `ama az s`a'at-e haft-e sobh t`a s`a'at-e shesh sh`am b`az ast.
The public library is open from seven in the morning until six in the
evening.

Months of the Year

There are twelve months in the Afghan calendar. The Afghan calendar is based on the solar system and is called شمسی هجری *Hijri Shamsi*. To convert the Afghan calendar date to the Christian calendar you add 621 or 622 to the Afghan year. From mid جدی *Jaddi* to the end of حوت *Hoot* you add 622, for the remaining days of the year you add 621.

حمل	*Hamal*	March 21 – April 20
ثور	*Saur*	April 21 – May 20
جوزا	*Jawz`a*	May 21 – June 20
سرطان	*Sarat`an*	June 21 – July 20
اسد	*Asad*	July 21 – August 20
سنبله	*Sunbola*	August 21 – September 20
میزان	*Miz`an*	September 21 – October 20
عقرب	*Aqrab*	October 21 – November 20
قوس	*Qaws*	November 21 – December 20
جدی	*Jaddi*	December 21 – January 20
دلو	*Dalv*	January 21 – February 20
حوت	*Hoot*	February 21 – March 20

Vocabulary

شنبه	*shanbe*	Saturday
یکشنبه	*yak shanbe*	Sunday
دوشنبه	*du shanbe*	Monday
سه شنبه	*seh shanbe*	Tuesday
چهارشنبه	*chah`ar shanbe*	Wednesday
پنجشنبه	*panj shanbe*	Thursday
جمعه	*juma'*	Friday
سرویس	*sarw`is*	bus
ایستگاه سرویس	*eastg`ah-e sarw`is*	bus stop
ترک کردن	*tark kardan*	to leave
کارکردن	*k`ar kardan*	to work
کار	*k`ar*	work
وزارت معارف	*viz`arat-e ma''arif*	ministry of education
وزارت	*viz`arat*	ministry
شروع کردن	*shur`u'kardan*	to start

Lesson Twenty-Nine درس بیست و نهم

Seasons

Afghanistan has four seasons. حمل *Hamal* is the first month of the calendar year هجری *Hijri*. First day of حمل *Hamal* is the Afghan New Year's. New Year is called سال نو *s`al`i naw* and every year it falls on March 21. Afghans celebrate سال نو *s`al-e naw* and prepare special dishes. Most families prepare سبزی چلو *sabzi chalav.* سبزی *sabzi* is a dish made of spinach and چلو *chalav* is white rice, and normally they are served together. Afghans also bake special cookies called کلچه نوروزی *kolcha-e nawruzi.*

The four seasons in Afghanistan are:

بهار	*bah`ar*	spring
تابستان	*t`abest`an*	summer
پائیز or خزان	*khaz`an* or *p`a`iz*	fall
زمستان	*zemest`an*	winter

تمرین Exercise

Write the following Dari paragraph. Read as you write.

افغانستان چهار فصل دارد.   اول حمل روز اول فصل بهار است. افغانها
روز اول بهار یا روز نوروز را جشن میگیرند. ماه های سرطان، اسد، و سنبله
فصل تابستان است. در تابستان هوا گرم میشود. در بعضی از
مناطق افغانستان مکتب ها برای دو هفته در تابستان رخصت میشوند.
میزان، عقرب و قوس فصل خزان است. خزان کابل قشنگ است.
درخت ها رو به زردی میروند. جدی، دلو و حوت فصل زمستان است.

Translation:

Afghanistan has four seasons. The first day of *Hamal* is the first day of
spring. Afghans celebrate the first day of spring or *Nawruz*. The months
of *Sarat`an, Asad* and *Sunbola* is summer. The weather gets hot dur-
ing the summer. Schools close for two weeks in some areas in Afghanistan. *Miz`an, Aqrab* and *Qaws* is the fall season. Kabul is pretty in fall.
The trees turn yellow. The winter is during the months of *Jadi, Dalv*
and *Hoot*.

Vocabulary

نوروز	*nawruz*	first day of Afghan new year (March 21)
سال نو	*s`al-e naw*	new year
سبزی	*sabzi*	an Afghan dish made of spinach
چلو	*chalav*	an Afghan dish made of white rice
کلچه	*kolcha*	cookie
کلچه نوروزی	*kolcah-e nawruzi*	special cookies baked for New Year's Day
بهار	*bah`ar*	spring
تابستان	*t`abest`an*	summer
پائیز or خزان	*p`a`iz* or *khaz`an*[12]	fall
زمستان	*zemest`an*	winter
مناطق	*man`atiq*	areas

---

[12] خزان *khaz`an* and پائیز *p`a`iz* are used *interchangeably.*

Lesson Thirty درس سی ام

Time

پیش از چاشت	*pesh az ch`asht*	before noon
بعد از چاشت	*b'ad az ch`asht*	afternoon
صبح	*sobh*	morning
چاشت	*ch`asht*	noon
شام	*sh`am*	evening
شب	*shab*	night
ثانیه	*s`aniya*	second (time)
دقیقه	*daq`iqa*	minute
ساعت	*s`a'at*	hour
روز	*ruz*	day
هفته	*hafta*	week
ماه	*m`ah*	month
سال	*s`al*	year

یک بجه
yak baja   or
one o'clock

ساعت یک
s`a'at-e yak
one o'clock

یک ونیم بجه
yako neam baja   or
half past one

ساعت یک و نیم
s`a'at-e yako neam
half past one

دو بجه
du baja   or
two o'clock

ساعت دو
s`a'at-e du
two o'clock

سه بجه
seh baja   or
three o'clock

ساعت سه
s`a'at-e seh
three o'clock

چند بجه است؟   ساعت چند است؟
chand baja ast?   or   *s`a'at chand ast?*
What time is it?   What time is it?

چهار و بیست   *chah`aro bist*   4:20
نه و پنجاه   *nuho pinj`ah*   9:50
پنج بجه است.   *panj baja ast.*   It is five o'clock.
پانزده کم پنج است.   *p`anzdah kam panj ast.*   It is quarter to five.

چهار و چهل و پنج است.
ch`ahar   va chihilo-panj ast.
It is four forty-five.

من یک بجه خانه میروم.
man yak baja mayravam.
I go home at one o'clock.

من ساعت نه صبح یک ملاقات دارم.
man s`a'at nuh-e subh yak mul`aq`at d`aram.
I have an appointment at 9:00 a.m.

لطفاً من را در هوتل کابل به ساعت سه بعد از چاشت ملاقات کنید.
lotfan manr`a dar Hotel-e K`abul beh s`a'at se ba'd as chast
mul`aq`at kun`id.   Please meet me at the Kabul Hotel at 3:00 p.m.

من ترا ساعت چهار به دفتر خود میبینم.
man tr`a beh s`a'at chah`ar dar daftar-e khud maybenam.
I will see you at my office at four o'clock.

من ساعت نه صبح در دفتر هستم.
man s`a'at-e nuh-e sobh dar daftar hastam.
I am in my office at 9:00 a.m.

لطفآ به ساعت ده و نیم صبح به کتابخانه بیائید.
lotfan beh s`a'at-e dah va neam sobh beh kit`ab kh`ana bey`aid.
Please come to the library at 10:30 a.m.

Vocabulary

پیش	*pesh*	before
بعد	*b'ad*	after
صبح	*sobh*	morning
چاشت	*ch`asht*	noon
شام	*sh`am*	evening
شب	*shab*	night
ثانیه	*s`aniya*	second (time)
دقیقه	*daq`iqa*	minute
ساعت	*s`a'at*	hour
روز	*ruz*	day
کم	*kam*	less, few
خوردن	*khordan*	to eat
ملاقات	*mul`aq`at*	meet
ملاقات کردن	*mul`aq`at kardan*	to meet
هوتل	*hotel*	hotel
مصروف	*masr`uf*	busy
چند	*chand*	few, how much, how many
چند دقیقه	*chand daq`iqa*	few minutes

Lesson Thirty-One درس سی و یکم

Climate

هوا	*hav`a*	air, weather
ابر	*abr*	cloud
ابرآلود	*abr`al`ud*	cloudy
سرد	*sard*	cold
خشک	*khoshk*	dry
غبار	*ghob`ar*	fog
هوای تازه	*hav`a-e t`aza*	fresh air
گرم	*garm*	warm
مرطوب	*mart`ub*	humid
رطوبت	*rot`ubat*	humidity
یخ	*yakh*	ice or cold
الماسک	*alm`asak*	lightning
باران	*b`ar`an*	rain
بارانی	*b`ar`ani*	rainy
برف	*barf*	snow
طوفانی	*t`uf`ani*	stormy
آفتاب	*`aft`ab*	sun
آفتابی	*`aft`ab`i*	sunny
حرارت	*har`arat*	heat
رعد	*ra'd*	thunder
شمال	*sham`al*	wind

امروز هوا گرم است.
emruz hav`a garm ast
The weather is hot today.

من روز های بارانی را خوش دارم.
man ruz h`a-e b`ar`ani r`a khosh d`aram.
I like rainy days.

در زمستان در کابل برف میبارد.
dar zimmest`an dar K`abul barf mayb`arad.
It snows in Kabul in the winter.

دیروز آسمان ابر آلود بود.
d`iruz `asm`an abr`al`ud b`ud.
The sky was cloudy yesterday.

Vocabulary

هوا	*hav`a*	air, weather
هوا تازه	*hav`a-e t`aza*	fresh air
ابر	*abr*	cloud
ابر آلود	*abr `al`uld*	cloudy
سرد	*sard*	cold
خشک	*khoshk*	dry
غبار	*ghob`ar*	fog
گرم	*garm*	warm
مرطوب	*mart`ub*	humid
یخ	*yakh*	ice or cold
الماسک	*alm`asak*	lightning
رعد	*ra'd*	thunder
باران	*b`ar`an*	rain
باران باریدن	*b`ar`an b`aridan*	to rain
بارانی	*b`ar`ani*	rainy
برف	*barf*	snow
برف باریدن	*barf b`aridan*	to snow
طوفانی	*tuf`ani*	stormy
آفتاب	*`aft`ab*	sun
آفتابی	*`aft`abi*	sunny
حرارت	*har`arat*	heat
شمال	*sham`al*	wind
آسمان	*`asm`an*	sky

Lesson Thirty-Two درس سی و دوم

Colors

سیاه	sey`a	black
آبی	`abi	blue
نصواری	nasw`ari	brown
طلائی	tel`ahe	gold
سبز	sabz	green
خاکستری	kh`akestari	gray
خاکی	kh`aki	khaki
لیموئی	limuhe	lemon
نارنجی	n`arenji	orange
بانجانی	b`anj`ani	purple
سرخ	surkh	red
نقره ئی	noqrahe	silver
فیروزه ئی	firozahe	turquoise
سفید	safed	white
زرد	zard	yellow

دریشی سیاه	dresh`i-e sey`a	black suit
آسمان آبی	`asm`an-e `abi	blue sky
پرده تاریک	pardah-e t`ar`ik	dark curtain
چای سبز	ch`ai sabz	green tea
سیب سرخ	seb-e surkh	red apple
پیاز زرد	pey`az zard	yellow onion

Vocabulary

منزل	*manzil*	house
پشتی	*pushti*	cover
پیاز	*pey`az*	onion
پرده	*pardah*	curtain
چوکی	*chawk`i*	chair
آسمان	*`asm`am*	sky
دریشی	*dresh`i*	suit

Lesson Thirty-Three درس سی و سوم

Family

پدر	*pedar*	father
پدرکلان	*pedar kal`an*	grandfather
مادر	*m`ader*	mother
مادرکلان	*m`ader kal`an*	grandmother
خواهر	*khw`ahar*	sister
خواهرزاده	*khw`ahar z`ada*	sister's children (male or female)
برادر	*ber`adar*	brother
برادرزاده	*ber`ader z`ada*	brother's children (male or female)
ماما	*m`am`a*	uncle (mother's brother)
کاکا	*k`ak`a*	uncle (father's brother)
خاله	*kh`ala*	aunt (mother's sister)
عمه	*`ama*	aunt (father's sister)
خسر	*khosur*	father-in-law
خشو	*khoshu*	mother-in-law

او پدر شما است؟
o pader shom`a ast?
Is he your father?

بلی، او پدر من است.
bale, o pader-e man ast.
Yes, he is my father.

او مادر شما است؟
o m`ader-e shoma ast?
Is she your mother?

نه، او خاله من است.
ne, o kh`ala-e man ast.
No, she is my aunt.

او برادر شما است؟
o ber`ader shoma ast?
Is he your brother?

نه، او بچه کاکا من است.
ne, o bach-e k`ak`a-e man ast
No, he is my cousin.

او مادر من است.

o m`ader-e man ast.

She is my mother.

نام کاکا من علی است.

n`am-e k`ak`a-e man Ali ast.

My uncle's name is Ali.

خاله من این کتاب را برای من خرید.

kh`ala-e man `in kit`ab r`a bar`ay-e man kharid.

My aunt bought this book for me.

تمرین Exercise

Write the following Dari paragraph. Pronounce as you write.

شیبلا سه برادر دارد. او هر روز با برادران خود به مکتب میرود. شیبلا به صنف سوم است. مریم دختر کاکا شیبلا است. شیبلا و مریم رفیق هستند. هر روز بعد از مکتب با هم بازی میکنند.

Translation:

Sheila has three brothers. Everyday she goes to school with her brothers. Sheila is in third grade. Mariam is Sheila's cousin. Sheila and Mariam are friends. Everyday they play together after school.

Vocabulary

خشو	*khoshu*	mother-in-law
خسر	*khosur*	father-in-law
عمه	*`ama*	aunt (father's sister)
خاله	*kh`ala*	aunt (mother's sister)
پدرکلان	*pedar kal`an*	grandfather
مادر کلان	*m`ader kal`an*	grandmother

Part V

Greetings, Common Phrases, and Expressions

Note: This part can be used independently from the previous chapters if you are interested in learning commonly used words, phrases, and expressions. Start with Part I if you are interested in reading and writing the Dari language. Ignore the Dari writings if you are not interested in reading and writing but would like to learn the conversational Dari only.

Greeting Customs

Afghan men often shake hands when they say hello سلام *(sa 'lam)* and goodbye خداحافظ *(khod`a h`afiz)*. Close male friends and relatives sometimes hug each other, especially when they meet after a long time. Afghans usually introduce themselves by their first names. Some Afghans use their father's name as their last name.

Women rarely shake hands with men when they say hello and goodbye. If women shake hands with men, they may make the initial move. Often women kiss on cheeks when they greet other women. Women will not hug men, unless they are her close family members.

When You Need a Taxi

Most taxis in Afghanistan do not have a meter to indicate the charges. Normally passengers tell their destination to the driver who will tell them how much they would charge for the trip. Charges may vary from one taxi driver to another, but it should be close. If you are staying in a hotel, you can ask the front desk to call a taxi for you and get a price for your destination. If you would like to do it yourself you can stand on the street and signal an available taxi. When you approach the taxi, tell the driver your destination and the taxi driver will tell you how much he would charge.

Some of the commonly used phrases to hire a taxi are:

How much do you charge to go to the airport?
t`a maid`an-e hav`aey chand maygired?

تا میدان هوائی چند میگیرید؟

The charge is two hundred Afghanis.
du sad Afgh`ani megeram.

دو صد افغانی میگیرم

How much farther is it?   *cheqadar r`ah mandah?*   چقدر راه مانده؟

Please take me through Shar-e Naw.
lotfan az r`ah-e Shar-e Naw berawaid.

لطفاً از راه شهرنو بروید.

Please take me to Kabul Hotel.
lotfan mar`a beh Hotel-e K`abul bebarid.

لطفاً مرا به هوتل کابل ببرید.

Where can I get a taxi?   *taxi az koj`a begiram?*   تکسی از کجا بگیرم؟

Do you take one hundred Afghanis to Kabul University?
yak sad Afghani t`a Pohantun-e K`abul maygired?

یکصد افغانی تا پوهنتون کابل میگیرید؟

I will take one hundred eighty.
man yak sad va hasht`ad Afghani megiram.

من یکصد و هشتاد افغانی میگیرم.

Hotel

When you check into a hotel, you may use some of the following phrases. For example, Mr. Thomas Brown wants to check into a hotel and speaks with the front desk clerk.

Mr. Brown: Hello, I have reserved a room.
sal`am, man yak utaq reserve karda am.

سلام، من یک اطاق ریزرو کرده ام.

Clerk: What is your name please?
lotfan n`am-e shom`a cheast?

لطفآ نام شما چیست؟

Mr. Brown: My name is Thomas Brown.
n`am-e man Thomas Brown ast.

نام من تامس برون است.

Clerk: Yes, I have your reservation, it is for one night.
bale, reservation shom`a r`a d`aram, baray-e yak shab ast.

بلی، ریزویشن شما را دارم. برای یک شب است.

Mr. Brown: Yes, I am staying for one night.
bale, man bar`ay-e yak shab meb`asham.

بلی، من برای یک شب میباشم.

Clerk: Would you like to check in now?
h`ale mekhwah`id keh ragister kunid?

حالا می خواهید که راجستر کنید؟

Mr. Brown: Yes, please check me in.
bale, lotfan mara ragister kun`id.

بلی، لطفـا من را راجستر کنید.

Clerk: Do you have your luggage with you?
baxh`a-e t`an hamr`ah-e t`an ast?

بکس ها تان همرای تان است؟

Mr. Brown: No, I left my luggage in the car. Please help me.
ne, baxh`a-e man dar motar ast. lotfan ma r`a komak kun`id.

نه، بکس ها من در موتر است. لطفا مرا کمک کنید.

Clerk: I will help you with your luggage.
man shom`a r`a b`a baxh`a-e t`an komak mekunam.

من شما را با بکس ها تا کمک میکنم.

Mr. Brown: Thank you.   *tashakor.*   تشکر.

Clerk: I have checked you in. Your room is on the fourth floor. Your
room number is 404. Here is your room key.
man shom`a r`a ragister kardum. ut`aq t`an dar manzil-e chaharum ast.
numrah-e ut`aq-e t`an 404 ast. i'n kele ut`aq t`an ast.

من شما را راجستر کردم. اطاق شما در منزل چهارم است.
نمره اطاق تان ۴۰۴ است. این کلید اطاق تان است.

Mr. Brown: Thank you very much.
besy`ar tashakor.

بسیار تشکر.

Additional questions that you may wish to ask at the front desk:

I would like a single room.
man ut`aq-e yak nafara mekhw`aham.

من یک اطاق یک نفره میخواهم.

I would like a double room.
man ut`aq-e d`u nafara mekhw`aham

من اطاق دو نفره می خواهم.

I would like a room for tonight.
man baray-e emshab yak ut`aq mekhw`aham.

من برای امشب یک اطاق میخواهم.

Do you have a room for one?
ut`aq-e yak nafara darid?

اطاق یکنفره دارید؟

What is the rate for one night?
qimat-e yak sab chand ast?

قیمت یک شب چند است؟

I need a room for one week.
man yak ut`aq baray-e yak hafta mekhwaham.

من یک اطاق برای یک هفته میخواهم.

Questions that Start with
What, Where, When, and Who

In Dari چه *che* (what), کجا *koj`a* (where), کی *k`i* (who), and کی *kai*[13] (when) do not come at the beginning of a sentence as in English, they come before the verb. Following are some examples of questions that start with what, where, when, and who.

Who is this?
`in k`i ast?
این کی است؟

When did Sheila come?
Sheila kai `amad?
شیلا کی آمد؟

What is your name?
n`am-e shoma che ast?
نام شما چه است؟

What is this?
`in che ast?
این چه است؟

What is your phone number?
numrah-e telefon-e shom`a che ast?
نمره تلیفون شما چه است؟

Where did you come from?
shom`a az koj`a `amada ayed?
شما از کجا امده اید؟

---

[13] کی *kai* and کی k`i are written alike in Dari. The difference between them is in their pronunciations and in their meanings.

Where do you work?
shom`a koj`a k`ar mekon`id?

شما کجا کار میکنید؟

Where is your house?
kh`ana-e shom`a koj`a ast?

خانه شما کجا است؟

Where are you from?
shom`a az koj`a hast`id?

شما از کجا هستید؟

Where is your pen?
qalam-e shom`a koj`a ast?

قلم شما کجا است؟

Who is your teacher?
mu'alim shom`a k`i ast?

معلم شما کی است؟

Who took your book?
kit`ab-e shom`a r`a k`i gereft?

کتاب شما را کی گرفت؟

Who came?
k`i `amad?

کی آمد؟

Who is this man?
`in mard k`i ast?

این مرد کی است؟

Commonly Used Words and Phrases

all day
tam`am-e ruz
تمام روز

Are you alone?
shom`a tanh`a hastid?
شما تنها هستید؟

Are you together?
shom`a b`aham hastid?
شما باهم هستید؟

Bon appetit!
noshej`an!
نوشجان!

day after tomorrow
pas fard`a
پس فردا

Do you speak English?
shom`a Inglisi gap mezanied?
شما انگلیسی گپ میزنید؟

For no reason.
bed`un-e dalil
بدون دلیل

Good bye.
khod`a hafiz*, or *b`am`an-e khod`a.
خداحافظ or بامان خدا.

Good luck.
muafaq b`ashid.
موفق باشید.

Good morning.
subh bakhair.
صبح بخیر.

Good night.
shab bakhair.
شب بخیر.

Hello.
sal`am.
سلام.

Hope to see you again.
*omaidw`aram shom`a r`a dub`ara
beb`iname.*
امیدوارم شما را دوباره ببینیم.

How are you?
chetoor hasti?
چطور هستی؟

How much is this?
`in chand ast?
این چند است؟

I am a student.
man sh`agird hastam.
من شاگرد هستم.

I am an American.
man Amrik`aey hastam.
من امریکایی هستم.

I am a tourist.
man tourist hastam.
من توریست هستم.

I am cold.
man sard hastam.
من سرد هستم.

I am fine.
man kh`ub hastam.
من خوب هستم.

I am from America.
man az Amr`ik`a hastam.

من از امریکا هستم

I came from Herat.
man az Herat `amada am.

من از هرات آمده ام.

I got wet in the rain.
man dar b`ar`an tar shodam.

من در باران تر شدم.

I like cold weather.
man hav`a-e sard r`a khosh d`aram.

من هوا سرد را خوش دارم.

I would like to...
man mekhw`aham ke...

من میخواهم که

It will be cold tomorrow.
fard`a sard ast.

فردا سرد است.

It is cold today.
emruz sard ast.

امروز سرد است.

It is hot today.
emruz garm ast.

امروز گرم است.

It is raining.
b`ar`an meb`arad.

باران می بارد.

It is rainy.
b`ar`ani ast.

بارانی است.

It is snowing.
barf meb`arad.

برف می بارد.

It rained yesterday.
diruz b`ar`an b`arid.

دیروز باران بارید.

It snowed yesterday.
diruz barf b`arid.

دیروز برف بارید.

It was cold yesterday.
diruz sard b`ud.

دیروز سرد بود.

luggage
baxh`a

بکس ها

kitchen
k`ar kh`ana or *`ashpazkh`ana*

کارخانه or آشپزخانه

last night
dishab

دیشب

my luggage
baxh`a-e man

بکس های من

My name is Sheila.
n`am-e man Sheila ast.

نام من شیلا است

next week
hafta-e `ayenda

هفته آینده

passport
passport
پاسپورت

please
lotfan
لطفاً

Please give me my check.
Lotfan bill mar`a bedehid.
لطفاً بل مرا بدهید.

Please sit down.
lotfan benishenid
لطفاً بنشینید

purpose of trip
hadaf-e mus`afirat
هدف مسافرت

safe trip
safar-e bekhatar
سفر بخیر

Sorry.
Mutasifam.
متأسفم.

Sorry for the misunderstanding.
az ghalat fahmi ma'zerat mekhw`aham.
از غلط فهمی معذرت میخواهم.

Thank you.
tashakor.
تشکر.

The sky is clear.
`asm`an s`af ast.
آسمان صاف است.

This is my passport.
`in passport man ast.
این پاسپورت من است

this week
`in hafta
این هفته

tonight
emshab
امشب

tomorrow
fard`a
فردا

tomorrow morning
fard`a subh
فردا صبح

tourist
tourist
توریست

tourist visa
visa-e touristi
ویزه توریستی

very good
besy`ar khub
بسیار خوب

Welcome.
khosh `amadid.
خوش آمدید.

The City

airport	*maid`an-e hav`aey*	میدان هوائی
bakery	*n`an w`aey*	نانوائی
bank	*b`ank*	بانک
barber	*dalok* or *salmani*	دلاک or سلمانی
bazaar	*b`az`ar*	بازار
bookstore	*kit`ab foroshi*	کتابفروشی
bus	*sarw`is*	سرویس
butcher	*qas`ab*	قصاب
car	*motar*	موتر
cinema	*cinem`a*	سینما
city	*shahr*	شهر
dry cleaning	*khushka shoei*	خشکه شوئی
factory	*f"abrika*	فابریکه
hospital	*shaf`akh`ana*	شفاخانه
hotel	*hotel*	هوتل
library	*kit`ab kh`ana*	کتابخانه
park	*p`ark*	پارک
pharmacy	*daw`akh`ana*	دوا خانه
police station	*mamuriyat-e police*	ماموریت پولیس
post office	*posta kh`ana*	پوسته خانه
restaurant	*restaurant*	رستورانت
school	*maktab*	مکتب
side walk	*pey`ada rav*	پیاده رو
stadium	*stadium*	ستودیم
store	*dok`an*	دکان
street	*sarak*	سرک
tailor	*khay`at*	خیاط
taxi	*taxi*	تکسی
traffic light	*cher`agh-e tr`af`ik*	چراغ ترافیک
university	*pohant`un*	پوهنتون
zoo	*b`agh-e wahsh*	باغ وحش

Health

ache	*dard*	درد
ambulance	*ambulance*	امبولانس
bandage	*bandazh*	بنداژ
blood	*kh`un*	خون
blood pressure	*fish`ar-e kh`un*	فشار خون
cancer	*sarat`an*	سرطان
cold	*rezish*	ریزش
cough	*surfa*	سرفه
dentist	*doktar-e dand`an*	داکتردندان
diarrhea	*ash`al*	اسهال
diabetes	*maraz-e shakar*	مرض شکر
disease	*maraz*	مرض
dizziness	*sar charkhi*	سرچرخی
doctor	*doktar*	داکتر
emergency	*`ajel*	عاجل
examination	*m`a'ena*	معاینه
faint	*zo'f*	ضعف
fever	*tab*	تب [14]
headache	*sardard*	سردرد
heart attack	*hamla-e qalbi*	حمله قلبی
hospital	*shaf`akh`ana*	شفاخانه
ill	*mar`iz*	مرض
illness	*mar`iz`i*	مریضی
injection	*pichk`ari*	پیچکاری
laboratory	*l`abratw`ar*	لابراتوار
malaria	*mal`ari`a*	ملاریا
measles	*surkhak`an*	سرخکان
medicine	*daw`a*	دوا
nurse	*parast`ar*	پرستار
operation	*`amaliy`at*	عملیات
optician	*`ainak saz*	عینک ساز
pain	*dard*	درد
patient	*mariez*	مریض

---

[14] *tav* تو is used in conversational Dari.

pharmacy	*daw`a kh`ana*	دوا خانه
pill	*goli* or *tablet*	کولی or تابلیت
prescription	*nuskha*	نسخه
rash	*bokhar*	بخار
sick	*mar`iz*	مریض
smallpox	*chichak*	چیچک
sneeze	*`atsa*	عطسه
sore throat	*gl`u dard*	گلون درد
surgeon	*jar`ah*	جراح
surgery	*jar`ahi*	جراحی
toothache	*dand`an dard*	دندان درد
vomit	*astifraq*	استفراق
whooping cough	*sey`a surfa*	سپاه سرفه
x-ray	*x-ray*	اکسری

Food and Meals

bread	*n`an*	نان
breakfast	*ch`ai sobh*	چای صبح
butter	*maska*	مسکه
cake	*cake*	کیک
cheese	*pan`ir*	پنیر
cookie	*kolcha*	کلچه
dinner	*n`an-e shab*	نان شب
egg	*tokhm*	تخم
food	*ghez`a*	غذا
honey	*`asal*	عسل
ice cream	*sheer yakh*	شیریخ
jam	*murab`a*	مربا
lunch	*n`an-e ch`asht*	نان چاشت
rice	*berinj*	برنج
salad	*sal`ad*	سلاد
salt	*namak*	نمک
soup	*shorb`a*	شوربا
stew	*qorma*	قورمه
yogurt	*m`ast*	ماست

Beverages

coffee	*qahwa*	قهوه
milk	*sheer*	شیر
tea	*chai*	چای
water	*`ab*	آب
yogurt drink	*dogh*	دوغ
green tea	*ch`ai-e sabz*	چای سبز
black tea	*ch`ai-e sey`a*	چای سیاه

Fruits and Nuts

almond	*b`ad`am*	بادام
apple	*seb*	سیب
apricot	*zard`al`u*	زردالو
banana	*kela*	کیله
dates	*khorm`a*	خرما
grape	*angoor*	انگور
lemon	*lim`u*	لیمو
melon	*kharb`uza*	خربوزه
mulberry	*t`ut*	توت
orange	*m`alta*	مالته
pear	*n`ak*	ناک
pine nut	*jalghoza*	جلغوزه
pistachio	*pista*	پسته
pomegranate	*an`ar*	انار
raisin	*kishmish*	کشمش
tangelo	*santara*	سنتره
walnut	*ch`armaghz*	چارمغز
watermelon	*tarb`uz*	تربوز

Vegetables

English	Transliteration	Dari
bean	*lobiy`a*	لوبیا
cabbage	*karam*	کرم
carrot	*zardak*	زردک
cauliflower	*gulp`i*	گلپی
corn	*jaw`ari*	جواری
cucumber	*b`adrang*	بادرنگ
eggplant	*b`anj`an-e sey`a*	بادنجان سیاه
garlic	*seer*	سیر
onion	*pey`az*	پیاز
pea	*nakhud*	نخود
pepper	*murch*	مرچ
potato	*kach`al`u*	کچالو
pumpkin	*kad`u*	کدو
reddish	*muli*	ملی
spinach	*sabzi*	سبزی
tomato	*b`anj`an-e r`umi*	بادنجان رومی
turnip	*shalqam*	شلغم

Meat

beef	*gosht-e gaw*	کوشت گاو
chicken	*gosht-e murgh*	کوشت مرغ
fish	*m`ahee*	ماهی
lamb	*gosht-e gosfand*	کوشت کوسفند
meat	*gosht*	کوشت
turkey	*gosht-e feelmurgh*	کوشت فیلمرغ

Clothing

baggy pants	*tunb`an*	تنبان
blouse	*b`al`atana*	بالاتنه
boots	*moza*	موزه
dress	*k`al`a, lib`as*	کالا، لباس
hat	*kola*	کلاه
jacket	*korti*	کرتی
pants	*patloon*	پطلون
scarf	*chadar*	چادر
shirt	*per`ahan*	پیراهن
shoes	*boot*	بوت
skirt	*d`aman*	دامن
socks	*jur`ab*	جراب
sweater	*j`akat*	جاکت
tennis shoes	*kirmich*	کرمچ
turban	*lung`i*	لنگی
veil	*ch`adari*	چادری

House

English	Transliteration	Dari
bathroom	*tashn`ab*	تشناب
bedroom	*ut`aq-e khw`ab*	اطاق خواب
blanket	*kampal*	کمپل
bookcase	*alm`ari-e kit`ab*	الماری کتاب
ceiling	*chat*	چت
chair	*chawk`i*	چوکی
corridor	*dahlaiz*	دهلیز
cup	*pey`ala*	پیاله
cupboard	*alm`ari*	الماری
curtain	*pardah*	پرده
dining room	*ut`aq-e n`an*	اطاق نان
door	*darw`aza*	دروازه
fan	*pakah*	پکه
fork	*panja*	پنجه
garage	*garage*	گراج
glass	*glass*	گلاس
guest room	*mehm`an kh`ana*	مهمانخانه
key	*kelid*	کلید
kitchen	*k`ar kh`ana* or *`ashpazkh`ana*	کارخانه [15]
knife	*ch`aq`u*	چاقو
lamp	*cher`agh*	چراغ
living room	*ut`aq-e sheshtani*	اطاق شیشتنی
lock	*qufl*	قفل
mirror	*`ayena*	آینه
oven	*d`ash*	داش
pitcher	*jug*	جگ
plate	*beshq`ab*	بشقاب
pot	*zarf*	ظرف
refrigerator	*yakhch`al*	یخچال
rug	*q`al`in*	قالین
shampoo	*shampoo*	شامپو
soap	*saboon*	صابون
sofa	*kawch*	کوچ

---

[15] Also called آشپزخانه.

spoon	*q`ashuq*	قاشق
stove	*bukh`ari*	بخاری
table	*maiz*	میز
towel	*ruep`ak*	روی پاک
wall	*diw`ar*	دیوار
window	*kilkeen*	کلکین
yard	*hawaili*	حویلی

English-Dari
Glossary

English	Pronunciation	Dari
about	*darb`arah*	درباره
ache	*dard*	درد
afghani (unit of money)	*afgh`ani*	افغانی
after	*ba`d*	بعد
afternoon	*ba`d az ch`asht* or *zuhr*	بعد از چاشت or ظهر
again	*dub`ara*	دوباره
against	*zid*	ضد
air	*hav`a*	هوا
airport	*maid`an-e hav`aey*	میدان هوائی
all	*hamah* or *tam`am*	همه or تمام
almond	*b`ad`am*	بادام
alone	*tanh`a*	تنها
ambulance	*ambulance*	امبولانس
America	*amr`ik`a*	امریکا
American	*amr`ik`aey*	امریکائی
ancestors	*ajd`ad*	اجداد
and	*va*	و
ant	*morcha*	مورچه
apple	*seb*	سیب
appointment	*mul`aq`at*	ملاقات
apricot	*zard`al`u*	زردآلو
area	*mantaqa*	منطقه
areas	*man`atiq*	مناطق
army	*lashkar*	لشکر
at	*beh*	به
aunt (father's sister)	*`ama*	عمه
aunt (mother's sister)	*kh`ala*	خاله
bad	*bad*	بد
baggy pants	*tunb`an*	تنبان
bakery	*n`anw`aey*	نانوائی
banana	*kela*	کیله
bandage	*band`azh*	بنداژ
bank	*b`ank*	بانک
barber	*dalok*	دلاک
bathroom	*tashn`ab*	تشناب
bazaar	*b`az`ar*	بازار
be	*budan*	بودن

English	Dari (transliteration)	Dari
bean	*lobiy`a*	لوبیا
bed (made of rope)	*ch`arp`aey*	چارپائی
bedroom	*ut`aq-e khw`ab*	اطاق خواب
beef	*gosht-e gaw*	گوشت گاو
before	*pesh*	پیش
beggar	*faq`ir*	فقیر
best	*kh`ubtar`in*	خوبترین
better	*kh`ubtar*	خوبتر
big	*kal`an*	کلان
bigger	*kal`antar*	کلانتر
biggest	*kal`antar`in*	کلانترین
bird	*parenda*	پرنده
black	*sey`a*	سیاه
blanket	*kampal*	کمپل
blood	*kh`un*	خون
blood pressure	*fishar-e kh`un*	فشارخون
blouse	*b`al`atana*	بالاتنه
blue	*`abi*	آبی
boat	*kishti*	کشتی
board	*takhta*	تخته
Bon appetit	*noshej`an*	نوشجان
book	*kit`ab*	کتاب
bookcase	*alm`ari-e kitab*	الماری کتاب
bookstore	*kit`ab foroshi*	کتاب فروشی
boots	*moza*	موزه
both	*hardu*	هردو
bought	*khar`id*	خرید
bowl	*k`asa*	کاسه
box	*sand`uq* or *bax*	صندوق or بکس
boy	*bacha*	بچه
bread	*n`an*	نان
breakfast	*ch`ai subh*	چای صبح
bring	*`awardan*	آوردن
brother	*ber`adar*	برادر
brother's children[16]	*ber`ader z`ada*	برادرزاده
brown	*nasw`ari*	نصواری

---

[16] Male or female

bus	*sarw`is*	سرویس
bus stop	*eastg`ah-e sarw`is*	ایستگاه سرویس
busy	*masr`uf*	مصروف
butcher	*qas`ab*	قصاب
butter	*maska*	مسکه
buy	*kharidan*	خریدن
cabbage	*karam*	کرم
cake	*cake*	کیک
came	*`amad*	آمد
camel	*shutur*	شتر
cancer	*saratan*	سرطان
capital	*p`aitakht*	پایتخت
car	*motar*	موتر
carpenter	*naj`ar*	نجار
carpet	*q`al`in*	قالین
carrot	*zardak*	زردک
cauliflower	*gulp`i*	گلپی
ceiling	*chat*	چت
chair	*chawk`i*	چوکی
chapter	*fasl*	فصل
cheese	*pan`ir*	پنیر
cherry	*`alub`alu*	آلوبالو
chicken	*murgh*	مرغ
children	*atf`"al*	اطفال
cinema	*cinema*	سینما
classroom	*sinf*	صنف
climate	*iqlim*	اقلیم
cloud	*abr*	ابر
cloudy	*abr`al`ud*	ابرآلود
coffee	*qahwa*	قهوه
cold (weather)	*sard*	سرد
cold (health)	*rezish*	ریزش
color	*rang*	رنگ
comb	*sh`anah*	شانه
come	*`amadan*	آمدن
condition	*ahw`al*	احوال
cookie	*kolcha*	کلچه
corn	*jaw`ari*	جواری

corridor	*dahlaiz*	دهلیز
cough	*surfa*	سرفه
cry	*girya*	گریه
cucumber	*b`adrang*	بادرنگ
cup	*pey`alah*	پیاله
cupboard	*alm`ari*	الماری
curtain	*pardah*	پرده
customs	*gomruk*	گمرک
cut	*bur`idan*	بریدن
damage	*nuqs* or *zarar*	نقص or ضرر
dark	*t`ar`ik*	تاریک
darker	*t`ar`iktar*	تاریکتر
darkest	*t`ar`iktar`in*	تاریکترین
dates	*khorm`a*	خرما
daughter	*dokhtar*	دختر
day	*ruz*	روز
decision	*tasmeem*	تصمیم
decree	*farm`an*	فرمان
dentist	*doktar-e dand`an*	داکتر دندان
diabetes	*maraz-e shakar*	مرض شکر
diarrhea	*ash`al*	اسهال
difficult	*mushkil*	مشکل
dining room	*ut`aq-e n`an*	اطاق نان
dinner	*n`an-e shab*	نان شب
direction	*taraf* or *dast`ur*	طرف or دستور
disease	*maraz*	مرض
divided	*taqs`im*	تقسیم
dizziness	*sar charkhi*	سرچرخی
doctor	*doktar*	داکتر
document	*sanad*	سند
dog	*sag*	سگ
donkey	*khar*	خر
door	*darw`aza* or *dar*	دروازه or در
dress	*k`al`a, lib`as*	کالا، لباس
dry	*khushk*	خشک
dry cleaning	*khushka shoei*	خشکه شوئی
easy	*`as`an*	آسان
eat	*khordan*	خوردن

edition	ch`ap	چاپ
egg	tokhm	تخم
eggplant	b`ang`an-e sey`a	بادنجان سیاه
eight	hasht	هشت
eighteen	hazhdah	هژده
eighth	hashtum	هشتم
eighty	hasht`ad	هشتاد
electricity	barq	برق
elephant	feel	فیل
eleven	y`azdah	یازده
emergency	`ajel	عاجل
English	inglisi	انگلیسی
entry visa	viza-e dukhool	ویزه دخول
equal	mas`awi	مساوی
escape	far`ar	فرار
evening	sh`am	شام
event	w`aqi`a	واقعه
every	har	هر
everyday	har ruz	هر روز
examination (health)	m`a`ena	معاینه
examination (school)	amteh`an,	امتحان
except	bed`un	بدون
exercise	tamr`in	تمرین
eyelashes	mizhg`an	مژگان
factory	f`abrika or k`arkh`ana	فابریکه or کارخانه
faint	zo`f	ضعف
fall	khaz`an	خزان
family	f`am`il	فامیل
fan	pakah	پکه
far	d`ur	دور
father	pedar	پدر
father-in-law	khosur	خسر
fever	tab	تب
few	chand	چند
fifteen	p`anzdah	پانزده
fifth	panjum	پنجم
fifty	pinj`ah	پنجاه
final	`akhir	آخر

fine	*kh`ub*	خوب
finish	*khal`as*	خلاص
fire	*`atish*	آتش
first	*avval*	اول
fish	*m`ahee*	ماهی
five	*panj*	پنج
flag	*bairaq*	بیرق
flight	*parw`az*	پرواز
flower	*gul*	گل
fly	*magas*	مگس
fog	*ghob`ar*	غبار
food	*ghez`a*	غذا
for	*baraye*	برای
fork	*panja*	پنجه
fortress	*dazh*	دژ
forty	*chehil*	چهل
four	*chah`ar*	چهار
fourteen	*chah`ardah*	چهارده
forth	*chah`arum*	چهارم
fraud	*taqalub*	تقلب
free	*muft*	مفت
fresh	*t`aza*	تازه
Friday	*juma`*	جمعه
friend	*dost*	دوست
from	*az*	از
fruit	*maywa*	میوه
future	*`ayenda*	آینده
garage	*gar`age*	گاراج
garden	*b`agh*	باغ
garlic	*seer*	سیر
gentleman	*`aq`a*	آقا
gentlemen	*`aq`ay`an*	آقایان
girl	*dokhtar*	دختر
give	*d`adan*	دادن
glass	*glass*	گیلاس
go	*raftan*	رفتن
gold (metal)	*tel`a*	طلا
gold (color)	*tel`ahe*	طلائی

goat	buz	بز
good	kh`ub	خوب
good bye	khud`a h`afiz	خداحافظ
grandfather	pedar kal`an	پدر کلان
grandmother	m`ader kal`an	مادرکلان
grape	angoor	انگور
gray	kh`akestari	خاکستری
green	sabz	سبز
guest	mehm`an	مهمان
guest room	mehm`an kh`ana	مهمان خانه
hail	zh`alah or z`ahah baridan	ژاله or ژاله باریدن
half	neam	نیم
hand	dast	دست
happy	khoshh`al	خوشحال
happier	khoshh`altar	خوشحالتر
happiest	khoshh`altar`in	خوشحالترین
has	d`arad	دارد
hat	kola	کلاه
have	d`ashtan	داشتن
he	o	او
head	sar	سر
headache	sar dard	سردرد
health	sehat	صحت
heat	har`arat	حرارت
heart	qalb, dil	قلب، دل
heart attack	hamla-e qalbi	حمله قلبی
hello	sal`am	سلام
help	komak	کمک
here	`inj`a	اینجا
high	baland	بلند
hill	tapah	تپه
hit	zadan	زدن
home	kh`ana	خانه
homework	k`ar-e kh`anagi	کار خانگی
honey	`asal	عسل
hope	omaid, omaidwar budan	امید، امیدواربودن
horse	asp	اسپ
hospital	shaf`akh`ana	شفاخانه

hot	d`agh	داغ
hotel	hotel	هوتل
hour	s`a`at	ساعت
house	kh`ana or manzil	خانه or منزل
how	chetoor	چطور
how much or how many	chand	چند
human	ins`an	انسان
humid	mart`ub	مرطوب
humidity	rot`ubat	رطوبت
hundred	sad	صد
I	man	من
ice	yakh	یخ
ice cream	sheer yakh	شیریخ
ill	mar`iz	مریض
illness	mar`iz`i	مریضی
in	dar	در
information	malum`at	معلومات
injection	pichk`ari	پیچکاری
inside	d`akhil	داخل
invite	da`wat	دعوت
is	ast	است
it	`in	این
jacket	korti	کرتی
jam	murab`a	مربا
journey	safar	سفر
key	kelid	کلید
khaki	kh`aki	خاکی
kind	mehrab`an	مهربان
king	sh`ah	شاه
kitchen	k`ar kh`ana, `ashpazkh`ana	کارخانه، آشپزخانه
knife	ch`aq`u	چاقو
knowledge	`ilm	علم
knowledgeable	f`azil	فاضل
laboratory	l`abratw`ar	لابراتوار
ladies	khanumh`a	خانم ها
lamb	gosht-e gosfand	گوشت گوسفند
lamp	cher`agh	چراغ
large	kal`an or bozurg	کلان or بزرگ

last night	dishab	ديشب
lazier	tanbaltar	تنبل تر
laziest	tanbaltar`in	تنبل ترین
lazy	tanbal	تنبل
leaf	barg	برگ
leave	tark kardan	ترک کردن
lemon (fruit)	lim`u	لیمو
lemon (color)	limuhe	لیموئی
less	kam	کم
lesson	dars	درس
letter	makt`ub or khat	مکتوب or خط
library	kit`abkh`ana	کتابخانه
life	zindagi	زندگی
lightning	almasak	الماسک
like	khosh dashtan	خوش داشتن
live	zindagi kardan	زندگی کردن
living room	ut`aq-e sheshtani	اطاق شیشتنی
load	b`ar	بار
lock	qufl	قفل
locust	malakh	ملخ
long	dar`az	دراز
lost	gom	گم
luggage	baxh`a	بکس ها
lunch	n`an-e ch`ash t	نان چاشت
malaria	mal`ari`a	ملاریا
man	mard	مرد
map	naqshah	نقشه
mark	asar	اثر
mask	neq`ab	نقاب
matches	gogird	گوگرد
mattress	toshak	توشک
me	man	من
meal	ghiz`a	غذا
measles	surkhak`an	سرخکان
meat	gosht	گوشت
medicine	daw`a	دوا
meet	mul`aq`at kardan	ملاقات کردن
melon	kharb`uza	خربوزه

men	mardh`a or mard`an	مردان or مردها
milk	sheer	شیر
ministry	viz`arat	وزارت
Ministry of Education	viz`arat-e ma`arif	وزارت معارف
minus	manfi	منفی
minute	daq`iqa	دقیقه
mirror	`ayena	آینه
mister	`aq`a	آقا
Monday	du shanbe	دوشنبه
money	paisa	پیسه
month	m`ah	ماه
moon	maht`ab	مهتاب
morning	sobh	صبح
most	besy`ari or aksaran	بسیاری or اکثراً
mother	m`ader	مادر
mother-in-law	khoshu	خشو
mouse	moosh	موش
much	ziy`ad	زیاد
mulberry	t`ut	توت
museum	muzium	موزیم
my	man	من
name	n`am or esm	نام or اسم
negative	manfi	منفی
neighbor	hams`aya	همسایه
new	naw	نو
New Year	s`al-e naw	سال نو
news	khabar	خبر
newspaper	akhb`ar	اخبار
next	`ayenda, digar	آینده، دگر
next to	pahlu	پهلو
next year	s`al-e `ayenda	سال آینده[17]
nice	kh`ub	خوب
night	shab	شب
nine	nuh	نه
nineteen	nuzdah	نزده
ninth	nuhum	نهم

---

[17] the word بسال bas`al is also used for next year.

ninety	*navad*	نود
no	*ne*	نه
noon	*ch`asht*	چاشت
nose	*b`ini*	بینی
notebook	*kit`abcha*	کتابچه
nothing	*haich*	هیچ
number	*numrah*	نمره
nurse	*parast`ar*	نرس
o'clock	*baja*	بجه
office	*daftar*	دفتر
often	*aksar*	اکثر
old	*pir*	پیر
on	*b`al`a, bar*	بالا، بر
one	*yak*	یک
onion	*pey`az*	پیاز
operation	*`amaliy`at*	عملیات
oppressed	*mazloom*	مظلوم
oppressor	*z`alim*	ظالم
optician	*`ainak s`az*	عینک ساز
or	*y`a*	یا
orange (fruit)	*m`altah*	مالته
orange (color)	*n`arenji*	نارنجی
origin	*manba`*	منبع
original	*asli*	اصلی
oven	*d`ash*	داش
over	*b`al`a*	بالا
page	*safha, waraq*	صفحه، ورق
pain	*dard*	درد
palace	*qasr*	قصر
pants	*patloon*	پطلون
paper	*k`aghaz*	کاغذ
park	*p`ark*	پارک
particle	*zarah*	ذره
pass	*gozashtan*	گذشتن
passenger	*mus`afir*	مسافر
passport	*passport*	پاسپورت
past	*gozashtah*	گذشته
patient	*mar`iz*	مریض

pea	*nakhud*	نخود
pear	*n`ak*	ناک
pen	*qalam*	قلم
pepper	*murch*	مرچ
percent	*f'isad*	فیصد
person	*nafar*	نفر
pharmacy	*daw`akh`ana*	دواخانه
physics	*fiz`ik*	فیزیک
pill	*goli* or *tablet*	گولی یا تابلیت
pillow	*b`alisht*	بالشت
pine nut	*jalghoza*	جلغوزه
pistachio	*pista*	پسته
pitcher	*jag*	جگ
plan	*pl`an*	پلان
plate	*beshq`ab*	بشقاب
please	*lotfan*	لطفاً
plus	*jama`*	جمع
police	*police*	پولیس
police station	*mamuriyat-e police*	ماموریت پولیس
pomegranate	*an`ar*	انار
post office	*posta kh`ana*	پوسته خانه
pot	*zarf*	ظرف
potato	*kach`al`u*	کچالو
preserving	*hifz*	حفظ
prescription	*nuskha*	نسخه
pretty	*maqbool*	مقبول
price	*nerkh* or *qimat*	نرخ or قیمت
print	*ch`ap* or *ch`ap kardan*	چاپ or چاپ کردن
problem	*mushkil* or *mas'ala*	مشکل
profit	*maf`ad*	مفاد
pumpkin	*kad`u*	کدو
purple	*b`anj`ani*	بانجانی
purpose	*hadaf, maqsad*	هدف، مقصد
quatrain	*rub`a`i*	رباعی [18]
question	*saw`al* or *mas'ala*	سوال or مسئله
radio	*r`adiyo*	رادیو

---

[18] a form of poem

rain	b`ar`an, b`ar`an b`aridan	باران ، باران باریدن
rainy	b`ar`ani	بارانی
raisin	kishmish	کشمش
rash	bokh`ar	بخار
read	khw`andan	خواندن
reason	dal`il	دلیل
red	surkh	سرخ
reddish	muli	ملی
refrigerator	yakhch`al	یخچال
relation	r`abetah	رابطه
restaurant	restaurant	رستورانت
rice	berinj	برنج
right	r`ast	راست
river	dary`a	دریا
road	sarak	سرک
roof	b`am	بام
room	ut`aq	اطاق
rubber	r`abar	رابر
rug	q`al`in	قالین
run	daw`idan	دویدن
sadness	gham	غمگین
safe	bekhatar	بیخطر
salad	sal`at, sal`ata	سلاد، سلاته
salt	namak	نمک
Saturday	shanbe	شنبه
saw	d`id	دید
say	guftan	گفتن
scarf	ch`adar	چادر
school	maktab	مکتب
scorpion	gazhdum	گژدم
season	fasl	فصل
second (time)	s`aniya	ثانیه
second (ordinal)	duvum	دوم
see	d`idan	دیدن
sell	furokhtan	فروختن
sentence	jumla	جمله
seven	haft	هفت
seventeen	haftdah	هفتده

English	Dari (transliteration)	Dari
seventh	*haftum*	هفتم
seventy	*haft`ad*	هفتاد
shampoo	*shampoo*	شامپو
she	*o*	او
shirt	*per`ahan*	پیراهن
shoes	*boot*	بوت
shop	*dok`an*	دکان
shopkeeper	*dok`and`ar*	دکاندار
short	*kot`ah*	کوتاه
shoulder	*sh`anah*	شانه
shovel	*beal*	بیل
sick	*mar`iz*	مریض
side	*taraf*	طرف
side walk	*pey`ada rav*	پیاده رو
silver (metal)	*nuqra*	نقره
silver (color)	*nuqrahe*	نقره ئی
single	*mujarad*	مجرد
sister	*khw`ahar*	خواهر
sister's children[19]	*khw`ahar z`ada*	خواهرزاده
sit	*nishastan*	نشستن
six	*shesh*	شش
sixteen	*sh`anzdah*	شانزده
sixth	*shashum*	ششم
sixty	*shast*	شصت
skirt	*d`aman*	دامن
sky	*`asm`an*	آسمان
sleep	*khw`ab*	خواب
small	*khord*	خورد
smallpox	*chichak*	چیچک
smell	*boe*	بوی
smoke	*d`ud*	دود
snake	*m`ar*	مار
sneeze	*`atsa*	عطسه
snow	*barf* or *barfb`aridan*	برف or برف باریدن
soap	*saboon*	صابون
sofa	*kawch*	کوچ

---

[19]   Male or female

solution	*hal*	حل
socks	*jur`ab*	جراب
son	*pesar* or *bacha*	بچه or پسر
sore throat	*gl`u dard*	گلودرد
sorry	*mutasif*	متآسف
soup	*shorb`a*	شوربا
source	*manba`*	منبع
speak	*harfzadan*	حرف زدن
spinach	*sabzi*	سبزی
spoon	*q`ashuq*	قاشق
spring	*bah`ar*	بهار
stadium	*stadium*	ستودیم
start	*shur`u` kardan*	شروع کردن
stew	*gorma*	قورمه
stocking	*jur`ab-e nylon*	جراب نیلون
store	*dok`an* or *magh`azah*	دکان or مغازه
storm	*t`uf`an*	طوفان
stormy	*t`uf`ani*	طوفانی
story	*qisa*	قصه
stove	*bukh`ari*	بخاری
street	*sarak*	سرک
student	*sh`agird*	شاگرد
sugar	*b`urah*	بوره
suit	*derashi*	دریشی
summer	*t`abest`an*	تابستان
sweet	*shireen*	شیرین
sun	*`aft`ab*	آفتاب
Sunday	*yak shanbe*	یکشنبه
sunny	*`aft`ab`i*	آفتابی
surgeon	*jar`ah*	جراح
surgery	*jar`ahi*	جراحی
sweater	*j`akat*	جاکت
table	*maiz*	میز
tailor	*khay`at*	خیاط
take	*gereftan*	گرفتن
talk	*gap zadan*	گپ زدن
tall	*baland*	بلند
tangelo	*santara*	سنتره

taste	*mazah*	مزه
taxi	*taksi*	تکسی
tea	*ch`ai*	چای
teach	*dar d`adan*	درس دادن
teacher	*mu`alim*	معلم
teapot	*ch`ainak*	چاینک
telephone	*telefon*	تلیفون
temperature	*har`arat*	حرارت
ten	*dah*	ده
tennis shoes	*kirmich*	کرمچ
tenth	*dahum*	دهم
than	*nisbat ba*	نسبت به
thank you	*tashakor*	تشکر
that	*`an*	آن
these	*`inh`a*	اینها
they	*`anh`a* or *aysh`an*	آنها or ایشان
think	*fikr kardan*	فکرکردن
third	*sehum*	سوم
thirsty	*tushna*	تشنه
thirteen	*sezdah*	سیزده
thirty	*see*	سی
this	*i`n*	این
those	*`anh`a*	آنها
thoughts	*afk`ar*	افکار
three	*seh*	سه
thousand	*haz`ar*	هزار
thunder	*ra'd*	رعد
Thursday	*panj shanbe*	پنجشنبه
ticket	*tiket*	تکت
time	*vaqt*	وقت
to	*beh*	به
today	*emruz*	امروز
together	*b`aham, yakj`a*	باهم، یکجا
tomato	*b`anj`an-e r`umi*	بادنجان رومی
tomorrow	*fard`a* or *saba*	فردا or صباح
tonight	*emshab*	امشب
took	*gereft*	گرفت
toothache	*dand`an dard*	دندان درد

torture	`az`ab	عذاب
tourist	tourist	توریست
toward	taraf	طرف
towel	ruep`ak	روی پاک
tower	burj	برج
traffic light	cher`agh-e tar`afik	چراغ ترافیک
traveler	mus`afir or rahguzar	مسافر or رهگذر
tribe	qabila	قبیله
trip	safar	سفر
Tuesday	se shanbe	سه شنبه
tulip	l`alah	لاله
turban	lung`i	لنگی
turkey	feelmurgh	فیلمرغ
turnip	shalgham	شلغم
turquoise	firozahe	فیروزه ئی
twelve	duv`azdah	دوازده
twenty	b`ist	بیست
two	du	دو
uncle (father's brother)	k`ak`a	کاکا
uncle (mother's brother)	m`am`a	ماما
under	zir	زیر
university	pohant`un	پوهنتون
us	m`a	ما
valley	w`adi	وادی
veil	ch`adari	چادری
very	besy`ar	بسیار
vinegar	sirka	سرکه
visit	mul`aq`at	ملاقات
visa	viza	ویزه
vomit	astifr`aq	استفراق
wall	diw`ar	دیوار
walnut	ch`armaghz	چارمغز
war	jang	جنگ
warm	garm	گرم
warmer	garmtar	گرمتر
warmest	garmtar`in	گرمترین
wash	shustan	شستن
watch	s`a`at	ساعت

water	`ab	آب
watermelon	tarb`uz	تربوز
we	m`a	ما
weapon	sal`ah	سلاح
weather	hav`a	هوا
Wednesday	chah`ar shanbe	چهار شنبه
week	hafta	هفته
welcome	khosh `amadid	خوش آمدید
well	khoob	خوب
went	raft	رفت
west	gharb	غرب
wet	tar	تر
what	che	چه
when	kai	کی
where	koj`a	کجا
which	kod`am	کدام
white	safed	سفید
who	k`i	کی
whooping cough	sey`a surfa	سیاه سرفه
will	khw`ahad	خواهد
wind	b`ad or sham`al	باد or شمال
windy	shamalak	شمالک
window	kilkeen	کلکین
wing	b`al	بال
winter	zemest`an	زمستان
with	b`a or hamr`ah	با or همراه
withered	pazhmurda	پژمرده
without	bed`un	بدون
wolf	gorg	گرگ
woman	zan	زن
women	zan h`a or zan`an	زنها or زنان
wood	chub	چوب
wool	pashm	پشم
work	k`ar or k`ar kardan	کار or کارکردن
world	dony`a	دنیا
write	navishtan	نوشتن
writing	khat, navishta	خط، نوشته
wrote	navisht	نوشت

x-ray	*x-ray*	اکسری
yard	*hawaili*	حویلی
year	*s`al*	سال
yellow	*zard*	زرد
yes	*bale*	بلی
yesterday	*d`iruz*	دیروز
yogurt	*m`ast*	ماست
yogurt drink	*dogh*	دوغ
you	*tu, shom`a*	تو، شما
zero	*sefer*	صفر
zoo	*b`agh-e wahsh*	باغ وحش

Other Hippocrene Dictionaries and Language Guides

AZERBAIJANI-ENGLISH/ENGLISH-AZERBAIJANI CONCISE DICTIONARY
8,000 entries • 144 pages • 5 ½ x 7 • ISBN 0-7818-0244-X • W • $14.95pb • (96)

**AZERBAIJANI-ENGLISH/ENGLISH-AZERBAIJANI
DICTIONARY & PHRASEBOOK**
4,000 entries • 176 pages • 3 ¾ x 7 • ISBN 0-7818-0684-4 • W • $11.95pb • (753)

FARSI-ENGLISH/ENGLISH-FARSI CONCISE DICTIONARY
8,000 entries • 250 pages • 4 x 6 • ISBN 0-7818-0860-X • $12.95pb • (260)

KURDISH-ENGLISH/ENGLISH-KURDISH DICTIONARY
8,000 entries • 313 pages • 4 ½ x 7 • ISBN 0-7818-0246-6 • W • $12.95pb • (218)

KYRGYZ-ENGLISH/ENGLISH-KYRGYZ CONCISE DICTIONARY
6,000 entries • 404 pages • 4 x 6 • ISBN 0-7818-0641-0 • W • $12.95pb • (717)

PASHTO-ENGLISH/ENGLISH-PASHTO DICTIONARY & PHRASEBOOK
3,000 entries • 235 pages • 3 ¾ x 7 • ISBN 0-7818-0972-X • W • $11.95pb • (429)

ENGLISH-PERSIAN STANDARD DICTIONARY
40,000 entries • 700 pages • ISBN 0-7818-0056-0 • $19.95pb • (365)

PERSIAN-ENGLISH STANDARD DICTIONARY
22,500 entries • 700 pages • 5 ½ x 8 ½ • ISBN 0-7818-0055-2 • $19.95pb • (350)

BEGINNER'S PERSIAN
288 pages • 5 ¼ x 8 ½ • ISBN 0-7818-0567-8 • $14.95pb • (696)

TAJIK-ENGLISH/ENGLISH-TAJIK DICTIONARY & PHRASEBOOK
1,400 entries • 148 pages • 3 ¾ x 7 • ISBN 0-7818-0662-3 • W • $11.95pb • (752)

URDU-ENGLISH/ENGLISH-URDU DICTIONARY & PHRASEBOOK
3,000 entries • 175 pages • 3 ¾ x 7 • ISBN 0-7818-0970-3 • W • $11.95pb • (427)

UZBEK-ENGLISH/ENGLISH-UZBEK DICTIONARY & PHRASEBOOK
3,000 entries • 225 pages • 3 ¾ x 7 • ISBN 0-7818-0959-2 • W • $11.95 • (166)

UZBEK-ENGLISH/ENGLISH-UZBEK CONCISE DICTIONARY
7,500 entries • 400 pages • 4 x 6 • ISBN 0-7818-0165-6 • W • $11.95 • (4)

Prices subject to change without prior notice.
To order **Hippocrene Books**, contact your local bookstore, visit
www.hippocrenebooks.com, call (718) 454-2366, or write to: Hippocrene Books, 171
Madison Avenue, New York, NY 10016. Please enclose check or money order adding
$5.00 shipping (UPS) for the first book and $.50 for each additional title.